ADELPHI
Paper • 306

Central European Civil–Military Reforms At Risk

Contents

Oxford University Press, Great Clarendon Street, Oxford OX2 6DP

Oxford New York

Athens Auckland Bangkok Bombay
Calcutta Cape Town Dar es Salaam Delhi
Florence Hong Kong Istanbul Karachi
Kuala Lumpur Madras Madrid Melbourne
Mexico City Nairobi Paris Singapore
Taipei Tokyo Toronto
and associated companies in
Berlin Ibadan

Oxford is a trade mark of Oxford University Press

Published in the United States
by Oxford University Press Inc., New York

© The International Institute for Strategic Studies 1996

First published December 1996 by Oxford University Press for
The International Institute for Strategic Studies
23 Tavistock Street, London WC2E 7NQ

Director: Dr John Chipman
Deputy Director: Rose Gottemoeller

British Library Cataloguing in Publication Data

Data available

Library of Congress Cataloguing in Publication Data

ISBN 0-19-829303-8
ISSN 0567-932X

INTRODUCTION

Civilian control of the military is one of the main requirements for Central European states to qualify for inclusion in NATO. Many Central European policy-makers believe that the civil–military reforms so far undertaken by these countries have already successfully met NATO's criteria. The Central European states – the Czech Republic, Hungary, Poland and Slovakia – have undoubtedly made progress in reforming their civil–military relations, but whether these reforms are now at a satisfactory stage or whether civilian control is still 'more a formality than a reality' remains to be seen.[1]

One of the dilemmas these states faced as they embarked on reform was whether to emphasise democratic or civilian control of the military. Historically, the two have been neither inseparable nor interdependent, nor has one proved more effective or ensured a more solid political structure than the other. This paper argues that control of the military has to be based on democratic foundations, and that in a pluralist democracy defence policy-making must be civilianised. These two notions have to be treated in tandem, almost as two sides of the same coin, if civilian control of the military is to become reality.

Democratisation, the introduction of basic democratic principles into security and defence policy-making, begins through legal means. This requires extensive legislative work and continuous refinement, but is relatively straightforward. It is also a relatively transparent process and easy to verify. The legal requirements of civil–military reform in Central Europe had on the whole been rather successfully met by 1993–94.

In these countries, civilianising security and defence policy-making, on the other hand, has been much less straightforward than democratisation. The objective difficulty of finding civilians expert in military matters has been one justification for the military retaining some control over defence policy-making. The process of civilianisation has also proved easier to reverse than democratisation, and more complicated to verify by outsiders. Yet it remains the condition for, and the guarantor of, the successful democratisation of security and defence policy-making. If civilianisation falls behind democratisation and civil–military reform relies not on elected members of parliament but on the non-elected military, the democratic principle itself risks being distorted and corrupted.

The security policies of the Central European states have been fundamentally re-oriented and in many ways reformed since 1989–90.

3

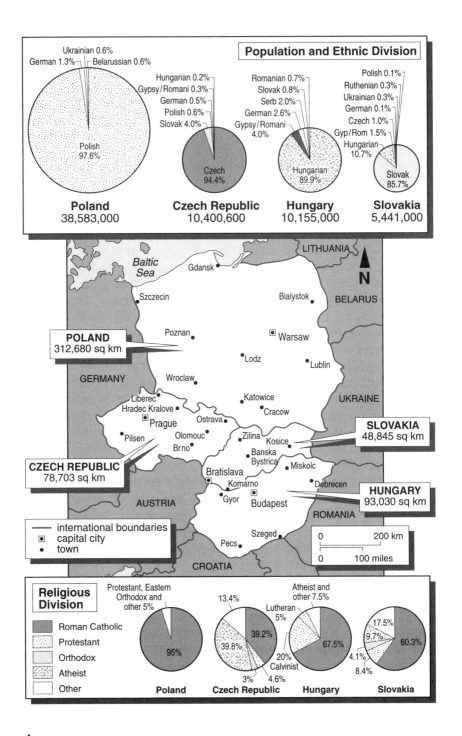

Population and Ethnic Division

Ukrainian 0.6%
German 1.3% — Belarussian 0.6%
Polish 97.6%

Poland
38,583,000

Hungarian 0.2%
Gypsy/Romani 0.3%
German 0.5%
Polish 0.6%
Slovak 4.0%
Czech 94.4%

Czech Republic
10,400,600

Romanian 0.7%
Slovak 0.8%
Serb 2.0%
German 2.6%
Gypsy/Romani 4.0%
Hungarian 89.9%

Hungary
10,155,000

Polish 0.1%
Ruthenian 0.3%
Ukrainian 0.3%
German 0.1%
Czech 1.0%
Gyp/Rom 1.5%
Hungarian 10.7%
Slovak 85.7%

Slovakia
5,441,000

LITHUANIA
N
Baltic Sea
Gdansk
Szczecin
Bialystok
BELARUS

POLAND
312,680 sq km

Poznan
Warsaw
Lodz
Lublin

GERMANY
Wroclaw
Liberec
Hradec Kralove
Prague
Ostrava
Pilsen
Olomouc
Zilina
Brno
Katowice
Cracow
UKRAINE

SLOVAKIA
48,845 sq km

Kosice
Banska Bystrica
Miskolc

CZECH REPUBLIC
78,703 sq km

Bratislava
Komarno
AUSTRIA
Gyor
Budapest
ROMANIA

HUNGARY
93,030 sq km

— international boundaries
☉ capital city
• town

Szeged
Pecs
Debrecen

0   200 km
0   100 miles

CROATIA

Religious Division

☐ Roman Catholic
▨ Protestant
☐ Orthodox
▨ Atheist
☐ Other

Protestant, Eastern Orthodox and other 5%
95%

Poland

13.4%
39.2%
39.8%
20%
3%   4.6%

Czech Republic

Atheist and other 7.5%
Lutheran 5%
67.5%
Calvinist
4.1%
8.4%

Hungary

17.5%
9.7%
60.3%

Slovakia

4

These changes have taken place in the face of domestic political and economic pressures, as well as against the backdrop of a profound transformation in the international security environment. As this paper's conclusion indicates, the interface between domestic and foreign policies in Central Europe has been a determining factor of civil–military reforms.

Immediately after the 1989–90 revolutions, the so-called Visegrád countries – Czechoslovakia (later to split into the Czech Republic and Slovakia) Hungary and Poland – were considered at the forefront of democratic reform. Since 1994, however, the pace of reform in these countries has begun to change. The Czech Republic, Hungary and Poland have continued to make substantial progress towards democratic civilian control of their militaries, as well as establishing functioning democracies and market economies and developing their civil societies. Political developments in Slovakia, however, have taken a different turn since the fall of Jozef Moravcik's government in October 1994 and Vladimir Meciar's electoral victory. Progress towards democracy and a market economy has been halted, and the country's civic society has begun to resemble that of Serbia rather than that of its neighbours.

In any country, the status of civil–military relations is inseparable from the democratic nature of the political and military elites. Civil–military relations can therefore be seen both as an indicator of, and a test for, reform in Central Europe. The degree of civilian control over the military is a good indication of the durability and stability of the new political structures, the depth of the democratisation process, and even the trend in political developments in the region. The stakes involved in civil–military reforms in Central Europe are thus both high and complex.

Given the different conditions in the four Central European states, this paper does not and cannot fully review their policies in the field of civil–military relations since 1989. Nor does it review the system of democratic accountability that has been set up to date.[2] Rather, this paper analyses why certain problems have occurred and/or persisted; what trends these indicate for the democratisation process; and what the implications of these trends are for the Western policy community. The analysis of the nature and causes of the problems confronted, as well as of policy developments in both Central Europe and the West, leads to the conclusion that many of the current reforms in Central Europe are becoming distorted. Establishing truly democratic civil–military relations in Central Europe is clearly at risk in the mid- to long term.

I. LAW AND INSTITUTIONS

The Division of Authority: Constitutional and Legal Reforms

Establishing the intricate web of relations and authority between legislative and executive, Prime Minister and President, and Minister of Defence and General Staff in post-Warsaw Pact Central Europe was bound to cause frictions. Creating new constitutional and legal frameworks prepared the way for the profound political re-orientation that has taken place in Central Europe since 1990. A democratic system has to be based on the rule of law, but constitutional reforms cannot in and of themselves guarantee a clear division of responsibilities. Instead, creating a system of accountability has had to involve:

- reforming the state structure proper by distributing power democratically among the three branches of government;
- reforming public administration into a professional and politically neutral civil-servant system;
- defining the interface between the military and political spheres and the role and function of the armed forces within the new democracies.

The armed forces may become involved politically for either of two reasons: the military itself may wish to participate in policy-making; or the political (civilian) actors may extend undue influence over the military. The former was a major focus of Central Europe's civil–military reforms. The latter was the driving force behind the policy of decommunisation in the first stage of reform after 1989–90. In the later stages, however, this policy had much less influence over the legal reforms, although the principle of sharing power among the branches of government was implemented practically throughout the region. Democratic legislation should, however, protect against both events.

On the one hand, those most involved in establishing civilian control of the armed forces tended to approach the issue in terms of opposing civilians to the military. In established democracies, there is rarely one united civilian approach to defence matters. Instead, civilians in one branch of government are continuously monitored and challenged by civilians in another. In practice, therefore, civilians control their fellow civilians before they control the military.

On the other hand, civilian control in Central Europe has all too often been simplified as subordinating the military to civilian authority. Yet a significant aspect of civilian participation in military matters involves coordinating and harmonising defence requirements with other national priorities. This requires a balance between civilian control, managerial efficiency and security.[1]

The civil–military reforms in Central Europe began with the elimination of the communist clauses in the countries' Constitutions and the establishment of a new chain of command and division of authority between President, parliament and General Staff. The reforms continued by strengthening the executive through appointing new Ministers of Defence and by beginning to civilianise the Ministries, as well as establishing the fiscal means to control and oversee the military. The order of priorities has been similar in all the Central and East European countries in transition from authoritarianism to democratic practices. The change in the relationship between civilian and military authorities and the end of the Communist Party's control of, and organised presence in, the military have been termed 'first order reforms'; alterations in the defence budget that reflect the existing boundaries between civilian and military authority have been called 'second order reforms'; and adjustments made to conform to the new priorities and to enhance effectiveness are known as 'third order reforms'.[2]

This is not to say that legislators, budgeteers or accountants could restrain the armed forces from making a decisive move into politics if they so wished. In any system, the military may see itself as the guardian of the spirit of the nation and thus as representing a higher authority. This becomes more likely if unstable, short-lived governments follow one another (as in Poland), if defence ministers are appointed in quick succession (as in Prague) or if the military perceives the civilian political sphere as incompetent (as practically throughout Central Europe). In the extreme, these circumstances increase the military's desire to impose its perception on the nation as a whole.[3] The non-Soviet Warsaw Pact countries did repeatedly use their militaries to crush internal unrest, for example in 1953 in Pilsen and Berlin; in 1956 in Poznan and Budapest; in 1969 in Prague; in 1970 in Gdansk; and in 1976 in Lodz and Warsaw. In all of these internal confrontations, however, only a minority of the armed forces ultimately defended the regimes.[4] In post-Cold War Central Europe, the major role legal measures play is to spread an institutional culture which, once developed, prevents the military exerting undue influence or abusing its power.

The post-1990 civil–military reforms faced many obstacles. One of the most intractable was that much of the administration of military matters under the communist system was not laid down in law. Instead,

7

the military's chain of command was assured primarily by nominating a loyal and trustworthy general as Minister of Defence. This nomination was then checked by the Central Committee of the Communist Party, which was closely linked to the Soviet Union through the then top-secret so-called Statute System. Marxism had its own concept of control over the military, and the Communist Party remained firmly in charge.[5] Pre-1989, the relationship between the Communist Party and the military had fluctuated. Under Khrushchev, the relationship was 'conflict-prone', and under Brezhnev 'participatory', 'symbiotic' or 'loosely coupled'.[6] Arguably, the Central European militaries were the partners and allies of the Communist Parties which intervened on their behalf – the military expressed far more reluctance to interfere directly than, for instance, the ministries of the interior which were under the Party's direct command.[7] While these communist constructs were by no means democratic, the military was controlled by civilian authority. The concept of political control of the military was thus not a new phenomenon post-1990. But irrespective of which of the above terms best describes the Cold War civil–military interaction in these countries, national militaries had to be brought back within the legal and institutional structures of their respective national societies after 1989.

The Executive

Destroying old channels of influence may have had its difficulties, but it has proved far easier than setting up new ones. Relations between Prime Minister and President have been one of the main causes of friction throughout Central Europe. As designated Commander-in-Chief of the armed forces, the President has direct access to the military high command. This responsibility has, however, been misinterpreted in some cases and has been distorted by other political priorities in the course of reforms.

Poland provides perhaps the best-known example of such frictions. From the *Sejm* and Senate elections in October 1991, President Lech Walesa's relationship with most successive governments and Ministers of Defence was tense, although for different reasons. Poland is not the only case. The intersection of political authority between President and Prime Minister has also been characterised by tensions in the other Central European countries. In the Czech Republic, President Vaclav Havel and Prime Minister Vaclav Klaus are two very different personalities with strongly opposing views on many issues which has resulted in a number of disagreements between them. In Slovakia, although President Michal Kovac was a co-founder of Prime Minister

Vladimir Meciar's Movement for a Democratic Slovakia (HZDS) and the two share a political background, since Slovakia's independence on 1 January 1993 tensions between Kovac and Meciar have increased rapidly to a state of virtual feud. In Hungary, parliament elected President Arpad Goncz in August 1990 from the parliamentary opposition to the first non-communist government, and in many ways he continued to act more as a member of the opposition than as an authority beyond party politics, throughout the first electoral period, 1990–94.

Although at the same levels of political authority, the frictions in these Central European states were channelled in different ways. In Poland, Walesa's political agenda was guided by the threat of the Communist Party returning to power. This primary concern relegated establishing democratic civil–military relations to a lesser position. Walesa made every effort to concentrate influence over military matters in the presidency – which he saw as the sole guarantor of protection against undue Communist Party influence over both the military and defence and foreign policy – even at the expense of the elected government and parliament. Since the Polish President is directly elected, presidential powers are not as purely symbolic as they are in the Czech Republic or Hungary. This made it even more difficult for other political actors to counter Walesa's efforts, even between December 1990 – when the former Communist Party (PUWR) lost power – and September 1993 – when its successor, the Democratic Left Alliance (SLD), came to power. While it is debatable whether Walesa was right about the way to fight the communists, he was right about the former Communist Party's return to power. From September 1993 onwards, the political situation in Warsaw was a *cohabitation à la Polonaise*, with one of the most anti-communist presidents in Central and Eastern Europe forced to work with the parliamentary majority of the former Communist Party.

In Hungary, the tense debate about political authority over the military was solved by the intervention of the third branch of government. The 1992 Constitutional Court ruling over peacetime authority clarified the situation by combining the posts of Commander of the Hungarian Army and Chief of the General Staff.

Although the views of Czech President Havel and Prime Minister Klaus have always significantly diverged, their differences have been kept behind closed doors. More important, Klaus' almost complete lack of interest in defence matters left Havel's presidential authority unchallenged and the stance of the executive towards the military

9

unambiguous. Since the Czech Republic's independence in 1993, presidential powers have gradually diminished in keeping with the new Constitution.

In Slovakia, the authoritarian nature of executive power has increasingly excluded 'presidential intrusion' in the Prime Minister's business. Successive budget slashes in the presidential office and President Kovac's *de facto* isolation from effective executive authority rendered Meciar's efforts to marginalise him successful.

Civilian oversight of the military should be a national policy effort and above party politics. All of the countries examined have thus in one way or another hindered attempts to establish civilian oversight of the military in Central Europe.

Civilianising the Ministries of Defence
Another major reform in Central Europe following the Constitutional changes was the civilianisation of the Ministries of Defence by appointing a Minister of Defence within the government with a defined role and position. The lack of civilian expertise in defence matters, however, created a serious dilemma for the newly elected governments. They could either select a Minister of Defence with democratic credentials, or one with knowledge of military issues.

In 1990, the freely elected Hungarian government opted for the former at the expense of the latter by appointing a civilian, Lajos Fur, as Minister of Defence. Civilianising both the Polish and Czech Ministries of Defence began with the appointment of civilian Deputy Ministers of Defence, Bronislaw Komorowski and Janusz Onyszkiewicz in Poland, and Antonin Rasek in the Czech Republic. Policy-makers in both countries chose to retain a career military officer as Minister of Defence for a transition period – Admiral Pjotr Kolodziejczyk and General Miroslav Vacek respectively – who would be acceptable to the military and politically reliable for the government. This was intended to ease the initial protests provoked by depoliticising the military. Yet in October 1990, Czech Minister of Defence Vacek was discovered to have been involved in activities against the 1989 revolution, and was replaced by the first civilian Czech Minister of Defence, Lubos Dobrovsky. The strengthening of Vladimir Meciar's power at the last Czech and Slovak federal elections in 1992 and the return to power of the former Communist Party in Hungary in 1994 introduced the practice of appointing retired military personnel to the post of Defence Minister. In Poland, the return of the former Communist SLD into the *Sejm* in September 1993 had the same effect.

Appointing civilian Deputy Ministers and Ministers of Defence may facilitate civilian control of the military, but it does not automatically guarantee effective civilian control. The new civilian Ministers of Defence also had to introduce a civilian presence lower down in the bureaucracy. What 'makes or breaks' effective civilian control of the Ministries of Defence is the effectiveness of their top-level political leadership and the efficiency of their professional administration.

Associates and Advisers
The new Ministers of Defence were criticised for their lack of technical military knowledge, distrusted by the older generation of the military, and faced with serious budgetary pressures. In addition, they were surrounded by a media hyper-sensitive to the eventual return of all-too familiar Cold War practices, such as misappropriations, tenders and contracts with civilian enterprises, or the abuse of public office. The senior leadership in the Ministries of Defence had to avoid a double danger: it could not consist exclusively of military personnel with one specific military approach, but the civilians' lack of military knowledge and insight risked rendering them uninfluential with no impact on decision-making. Both scenarios have been seen in Central Europe.[8]

In addition to their lack of knowledge of defence matters, some civilian Ministry of Defence staff had to overcome their antipathy towards the military ingrained by decades of political opposition to the communist regimes.[9] Moreover, it was not clear to the military staff whether the new civilian appointments were policy or civil service positions. Sometimes the new appointees showed aspects of both as personal relations influenced the nominations. As a result, the military staff tended to treat even the politically neutral appointments as if they were primarily political. Accustomed to the practices of the previous 40 years, this reaction is understandable, but inaccurate. Tensions between the new civilian policy-makers and military personnel, mutual misunderstanding and mistrust gradually created serious problems for the civilian leadership.

Administrative Efficiency
The bureaucratic mechanisms that implement top-level decisions, prepare the background work with other ministries, link the Minister of Defence's responsibilities to the military command and communicate the military's needs to the Minister are essential if civilian control is to be effective. Ministerial responsibility can be jeopardised or undermined by

a lack of public administrators or by their unprofessionalism and inefficiency.

Many of the problems associated with civilianising the Ministries of defence are common to all four Central European states. The increasing presence of civilians in the Ministries provoked an emotional reaction from the military in all these countries. Many military personnel perceived decisions made by the new political elite as party politics which seriously challenged deeply ingrained pre-1989 customs. As a result, many military staff in civil service positions, especially the older generation, felt that their personal attitudes and thinking were being threatened. For its part, the new political leadership in the ministries was largely unprepared for these bureaucratic complexities.

The resulting intra-ministerial tensions and bureaucratic intrigues proved more intense than expected. Indeed, the institutions that proved most resistant to administrative reform were, according to some experts, the Ministries of Defence themselves.[D] Public administration represented a somewhat unexpected challenge to civil–military reform in most Central European countries. Mid-level personnel retained their positions throughout the changes in regime. In the Ministries of Defence, where all positions had been filled by military personnel, staff in mid-level bureaucratic posts are most likely to mishandle implementing decisions, find their administrative expertise incompatible with the intentions of the high-level political leadership, and maintain or increase bureaucratic inefficiency. There is a fine line between simple administrative inertia and deliberately undermining the new administration. Problems of intra-ministerial coordination thus seriously hampered civil–military reform, which, in the words of one official became 'a risky venture on thin ice'.[11]

Civilianising defence policy-making is primarily a matter of political commitment, despite all the objective obstacles in its path. The background for these policies was particularly favourable in the Czech Republic after the so-called Velvet Revolution of 1989. Many officers who had left the military after 1968 for political reasons or who were discharged from service during the communist era, became actively involved in the political transition in 1989–90. In December 1989, they formed the military union *Obroda* ('Renewal') which later became part of the Civic Forum and played an important role in the Czech military's transition from a Warsaw Pact force to a national defence force. Although to many active military personnel the *Obroda* members were as 'alien' as the rest of the new political elite, more than one thousand

Obroda members returned to active positions in the Ministry of Defence, either as military personnel or as civilians.[12] After this first wave, a new and younger generation of civilians were appointed. Over time, the role of *Obroda* members in the Ministry became more indirect and gradually declined, but it was central in the first period of transition. The policy of hiring civilians in the Czech Ministry of Defence has continued. Some estimate that by 1996 the percentage of civilians working at all levels in the Ministry was more than 40%, and even the more modest figures are around 30%. Poland has also increased the number of civilians working in its Ministry of Defence, some as heads of departments and divisions with military personnel as their deputies. While this process has suffered from the frequent changes of government, it has nevertheless contributed to a tangible increase in the civilian presence in the Polish Ministry of Defence.

There is a marked difference between the presence of civilians in the Hungarian Ministry of Defence under the two post-1989 governments. Civilianisation at all levels was one of the stated and practised goals of Jozsef Antall's government in 1990–94. Following the general elections in 1994 and the return to power of the former communist government, however, this trend was halted and then reversed. Civilians remained only in support and junior positions, while the key decision-making positions were filled by the military, both retired and active. Developments in Hungary since then demonstrate what happens when the executive's commitment to civilianise the Ministry of Defence disappears. Although there are no legal obstacles to hiring civilians to top-level advisory positions, nor to the Minister of Defence's consultative body, of the five deputy state secretaries in the Ministry in 1996 only one was a civilian compared to four under Antall's government. This situation improved slightly as a result of Western pressure. A UK specialist team that studied the Ministry's policies in 1995 concluded that 'if civilianisation of senior Ministry of Defence posts is to take place and succeed, it *will require the endorsement* of the Government and the *commitment* of the Minister of Defence and the Defence Collegium' – commitment that the team could not detect.[13]

In Slovakia, the policy of civilianising the Ministry of Defence remains in doubt, and there is little evidence of any increase in civilian staff, and no policy has been introduced to change the situation. While young Slovak officers, especially those with some Western training, support the principle of democratic civilian control of the military, many of the older generation of military personnel in the Ministry of Defence emphasise their ability to revert to either a civilian or a military role as required at any time.

A major aspect of restructuring civil–military relations throughout Central Europe involved delineating a clear division of responsibility between the Minister of Defence and the General Staff. This relationship includes both peacetime and wartime command of the military, management of the defence budget, military intelligence and counter-intelligence, senior military promotions and appointments, equipment acquisition, force deployment, strategic planning and force structure. The problems encountered in this relationship reflect both the different military traditions and the diversity of the post-1989 political leadership in Central Europe. Despite the existence of a legal framework for civilian oversight of the military, decision-making practice shows that the military has managed to bypass civilian oversight either deliberately or by default in practically all four countries. None of these 'bypasses' threaten the political system of the states concerned, but they do again illustrate the difficulties inherent in implementing the reforms.

Poland: Infighting Among Political Players
However clear-cut the Constitutional terminology concerning the division of authority among the different political actors, its inter-pretation can still cause political infighting. In Poland, tensions heightened after 1993, leading President Walesa to declare to the *Sejm* in early 1995 that the 'military people should run the military' and to extend his powers to the maximum.[14] By the end of 1995, the Polish government had effectively lost control of the military. In this feud between parliament and President, however, the General Staff managed to play President and government off against each other. This infighting dominated Polish politics until the November 1995 presidential election when Aleksander Kwasniewski ousted Lech Walesa and unified the political front-line between parliament and government, both held by the former Communist Party. This made possible essential legislation which clarified the relationship between the Minister of Defence and the General Staff, with the result that the General Staff was incorporated into the Ministry of Defence. This created a radically new relationship between the Ministry of Defence and the General Staff – whose effectiveness is so far untested – unknown in all established Western democracies, but reminiscent of the old Soviet system.

The Czech Republic: Neglecting Key Political Actors
Lack of knowledge combined with lack of interest is not a stable foundation for effective democratic oversight of the military. A less frequently cited threat to effective civilian control is neglect of the military and military issues by civilian policy-makers. This neglect was evident in Czech policy-making soon after the initial stage of political reforms when the military was no longer perceived as a threat to the country, and interest in it declined rapidly. Few Czech members of parliament show any genuine interest in defence matters and, if they do, their interest focuses largely on one particular aspect of the military, not on overall issues of national security policy or defence restructuring. These parliamentarians also lack insight into how the military operates. Only President Havel has continued to fulfil his Constitutional duties to both the military and national security issues.

Although democratic powers were formally delegated to the Czech Minister of Defence after 1989, the General Staff has successfully developed and promoted its own ideas on military matters, sometimes at the expense of those developed by the civilian leadership (either in the Ministry of Defence or in parliament). One of the clearest examples of this is the debate about professionalising the Czech military. Most politicians supported the idea of a small military (40–45,000 personnel) with a high (75%) rate of professionalisation to be created by the end of the century. The Chief of the General Staff, however, proposed a larger (65,000 personnel) and less professionalised (50%) military in 1993, after the Czech Republic gained its independence. This latter concept finally became official policy.

Hungary: Bypassing Control Through Legal and Administrative Means
In Hungary, the Ministry of Defence and the General Staff are effectively two separate organisations. The institutional set-up renders the Minister of Defence and the recently established Defence Collegium – the Minister's advisory and consultative body – the exclusive common forum of the Ministry of Defence and the Home Defence Forces (HDF). The Minister thus has to run two almost parallel organisations. It is unlikely that he alone could effectively deal with all defence responsibilities. Some argue that this structure had been originally established by the outgoing communist government in 1990 to increase efficiency and was based on rational not political arguments. In reality, the decision seems to have been far more political, and its administrative effect has proved negative. The double structure means that any

15

initiative coming from either side has to work its way through both branches, causing overlap, duplication and inefficiency. The double structure also makes it very difficult for Western partners and NATO staff to identify their Hungarian counterpart, thus making the country's national policy goal of promoting Western integration more difficult.

The General Staff's continued *de facto* independence from the Ministry of Defence, however, has had visible repercussions. It perpetuates the old Warsaw Pact mentality that institutions outside the military, such as parliament, should have no effective role in military matters. For example, in spring 1996 eight Hungarian MiG-29s took part in a live-fire exercise in Poland without the parliamentary authorisation required by the Constitution and, as Minister of Defence Gyorgy Keleti claimed, without his prior knowledge either.

Slovakia: Continuing Pre-1989 Traditions
Although civilian control of the military is official policy in Slovakia, actual relations between the Ministry of Defence, the General Staff and parliament continue to follow pre-1989 patterns. A perceivable degree of defence policy-making occurs outside democratic institutions such as parliament, and a Warsaw Pact-type lack of interference by political institutions remains common practice.

The presence in the Ministry of Defence and the higher military ranks of a few young officers could have had a very positive influence on democratic thinking about defence. Yet authoritarian governmental policies prevail and hamper civil–military reforms as well. Given the lack of civilian experts in military matters and of genuine governmental commitment, civilianising defence policy-making in Slovakia remains largely rhetoric. Reforms have had only superficial success in the political system. Civilians can only be found in the legislative, but they remain largely ineffective because they lack specialist knowledge and non-military expert support. The result is a combination of: pre-1989 relations between the General Staff and the executive on the one hand, and a degree of military independence on the other; a lack of civilian presence within the executive; and a lack of political weight in the democratic institutions.

The Legislative
Parliament, the legislative branch of government, fulfils one of the 'prime requirements' for democratic civil–military relations through popular accountability.[16] It is empowered to merge legality with public

understanding and support for, or at a minimum acceptance of, the military. Parliament's fiscal powers merit an in-depth analysis of their own and are the subject of the next chapter, while this chapter focuses on parliament's legislative powers.

Many Central European experts believe that the newly restored parliaments were the institutions that adopted democratic characteristics the fastest. On the other hand, many Western experts claim that Central European parliaments are ineffective instruments of civilian control. This divergence of views can be explained by examining the different aspects of the legislative's work.

Formulating National Strategy and Doctrine
Following the changes in regime in Central Europe after 1989, parliaments have tangibly influenced the formulation of national defence policies. The strategic re-orientation of these countries took place after much non-partisan work by parliament and massive legislative changes in the Constitution and elsewhere which enabled reform to go ahead. High priority was also given to defining the role and place of the armed forces in society, determining their size, structure and strategic requirements, and identifying national defence priorities. Initially, the newly developed 'military doctrines', or 'defence concepts' as they were also known, provided this framework. Pressured by the changing international – and regional – security environment, all four Central European states had developed these documents by the end of 1993. The sole exception was the Czech Republic which, by autumn 1996, still had no formal military doctrine.

Accountability and Transparency
The legislative in Central Europe has also been influential in enforcing accountability of the executive. Its ability to infiltrate executive policy has been facilitated by Committee hearings and written reports. Parliaments have sustained and gradually – albeit slowly – increased their involvement in defence. A key area requiring accountability and transparency is financing defence. Parliaments have successfully held their governments accountable, if not in the detailed breakdown of the defence budget, at least in its overall figures.[15] In theory, the defence budget represents the electorate's most immediate contribution to defence, and parliament is responsible to the electorate. Under the stringent economic pressures created by the transition to market economies, governments had to justify their proposed defence budgets

that parliament would then allocate. This process has visibly increased transparency in defence procedures.

Another major area of transparency concerns parliamentary responsibility for keeping the military within the fabric of society and improving its public image. This broader dimension of civil–military relations is particularly important in the Central European states that have a 40-year tradition of separating the military from society, and that continue the practice of general conscription. A positive trend is parliaments' success in monitoring and improving conscripts' human rights and the atmosphere within the armed forces.[16] Setting the military within the political context of its country, however, so that it serves national political priorities and aims is a complex, long-term task which will require substantial parliamentary work over a long period.

Defining the Legislative Powers of Parliament
Defining the legislative powers of parliament in established democracies highlights how far they are from a cut-and-dried matter of civil–military relations: while the principle of the division of power indicates that legislation originates in parliament, in reality most legislative proposals come from the executive, in Western democracies as well. Detailed rules and regulations are not initiated by parliaments. Moreover, a large number of regulations relating to the military take the form of 'executive orders' from the Ministry of Defence, but have the power and effect of laws. Parliaments are not in practice public policy-makers. This is not a function of their legal competence, but of its practical limitations.[17] Instead, they act rather as a revisionary board. In terms of their practical competence, the legislative powers of the Central European parliaments have fared surprisingly well in the transition process.

Whether parliaments do actually affect the security and defence policy-making processes or merely endorse the outcome produced by the executive depends largely on the vigour and expertise of the Security and/or Defence Committees and the Budget Committees. In the West, the political practice of parliaments varies widely. The US Congress plays a highly intrusive role in policy-making and its influence has increased since the end of the Cold War. The German *Bundestag* also has a direct influence on policy. The UK and French parliaments, on the other hand, play a much less intrusive and more reactive role. During the 40 years of Soviet influence in Central and Eastern Europe, however, the only role parliaments played was a symbolic one, a legacy that is hard to change.

Parliamentary effectiveness depends on many factors, but is impossible without well-informed, knowledgeable members of parliament on the relevant parliamentary committees. In Central Europe, acquiring the requisite knowledge and information was not an easy task. In establishing civilian control of the military, relations between the executive and the legislative have often been tense and non-cooperative. The requirement that the General Staff or Ministry of Defence produce written reports has been controversial, and the executive has tended to view the parliamentary committees as irritating nuisances.[18] Access to information is still a complicated matter in most Central European countries. The military has a strong corporate identity which makes civilian 'intrusion' a sensitive issue, particularly in a region where neither civilians nor the military are accustomed to working together. In addition, members of parliamentary committees are not generally elected from their parties' elite and have often suffered from the lack of priority parliament has given to defence matters.

The Defence Committees can, however, become more expert. In Slovakia, former Minister of Defence Imrich Andrejcak was appointed Chairman of the Defence Committee; in Hungary, former Minister of Defence Fur and other former members of the Defence Committee were re-elected to parliament and then to the Committee after the 1994 general elections; and in Poland, former Minister of Defence Onyszkiewicz was appointed Chairman of the Defence Committee. In these cases, the Committees clearly gained expertise and insight into military matters, significantly enhancing the quality of their work and their effectiveness in strengthening civilian oversight, especially at a time when governmental commitment to the defence reforms was causing concern. In some cases, as in the Czech Republic, however, the Security Committee's responsibilities have been extended to cover policing issues, further limiting the time and attention parliament can devote to defence and military-security matters.

Conclusions

After the first half-decade of legislative reforms in Central Europe, the following conclusions can be drawn:

- Although some areas of divided or unclear authority over the military remain, although the various political actors have tended to over-expand their sphere of control, and although insubordinate personnel or a lack of intra-ministerial or intra-governmental coordination have on occasions impeded establishing fuller civilian control over the military, the legal framework for civilian oversight of the military is by and large complete in Central Europe.

- Central European Security and Defence Committees have not yet truly narrowed the gap with their Western counterparts. Yet, of the newly established democratic institutions in Central Europe, the legal competence of parliaments has come closest to that of Western legislatures, even though members of parliament lack sufficient information, resources, expert independent assistance and analysis, and, in some cases, even the authority of those in the West.
- Further legislative work in the field of civil–military relations must provide the missing legal links in clarifying command and control; refine existing legislation in the light of national experience after the first six years of reforms; and, most important, fill the existing legislative framework and make an impact on decision-making. The process of democratising civil–military relations cannot succeed without the endorsement and commitment of government. Until then, civilian influence over the military remains in many ways limited to, and limited within, the legislative in most of Central Europe.
- The policy of civilianisation has been strongly criticised for recruiting personnel with no expertise in defence matters. Yet, over time, civilianising the executive promises a double result: the expertise of those hired in the first wave will develop 'on the job'; and only a continued commitment to the policy can ensure that the number of civilians trained and educated in military matters gradually increases. Despite the mistakes made since 1990, this policy was testimony to the government's genuine commitment to democratic control of the military. There are, however, signs that the policy is now being shelved following political changes in many Central European countries.

II. FINANCIAL MEANS OF CIVILIAN OVERSIGHT

Establishing the legislative framework for civilian oversight of the military, although fundamental, is only a first step towards genuine reform. The 'power of the purse' is one of the most effective tools for civilian and parliamentary influence over defence and security policy-making. Controlling the defence budget is thus perhaps the most effective way of overseeing the military. Some, especially in the Czech Republic, have gone as far as to declare that this is practically the only aspect parliament really needs to control.[1]

In 1990, for the first time in four decades, military budgets in Central Europe were made public in a complete and broken-down form. Transparency in defence budgeting and budget planning has since become a fundamental goal of defence reforms. One of the first, and somewhat unexpected, obstacles facing the new political elite in increasing transparency was the military's lack of knowledge of actual costs and expenditures. Introducing cost-sensitivity into the military could only be done gradually, especially in the former Warsaw Pact states with their memories of the not-so-distant-past 'plenty', and developing cost-consciousness and eliminating waste of resources is a continuing process. Yet thinking in terms of limited resources has had a powerful and long-term impact on the mentality of those involved in defence matters.

The Fiscal Background to Civil–Military Reforms

The pressures attendant on the transitional economies – declining gross domestic product (GDP), high inflation and unemployment in most sectors – further aggravated the tensions inherent in reforming civil–military relations. Despite decreasing military budgets, defence reforms had to be implemented. The fall in GDP and economic output has traditionally been cited as the cause of the declining defence budget in Central Europe. Since 1993–94, however, these economies have begun to recover from the first phase of transition. In 1993, Poland was the first former Council for Mutual Economic Assistance (COMECON) country to register economic growth, and the Czech Republic, Hungary and Slovakia followed suit in 1994. Yet this did not automatically reverse the decline in the defence budget since economic growth alone has no effect on the share of gross national product (GNP) allocated to the defence budget.

This trend was only reversed as a result of the Central European policy goal of integration into Western security structures. Where there was the political will a fiscal way could be found as continued economic growth allowed for an increase in the defence budget's share of GDP. In both Poland and the Czech Republic, the defence budget's share of GNP has increased to 3% for 1997. In Poland, where the economy is predicted to grow by about 6–7% in 1997, this is a significant rise. In both countries, increasing the defence expenditure to 3% is a parliamentary expression of their commitment to join NATO. The Hungarian military budget, on the other hand, had fallen to a devastating low by 1996. The economic growth that began in 1993–94 did not continue at the same rate as Hungary's Central European neighbours in 1995. Inflation has steadily increased and economic pressures have risen, further depressing the defence budget for 1997. As a result, the Hungarian military has been forced to use up all its reserve supplies, and by 1997 even its mobilisation supplies will have been exhausted. Of the four examined, the Hungarian military is also in most immediate need of new technology. Most of its army vehicles are more than 20 years old and the number of accidents caused by their decrepit state has increased since 1994. Under these circumstances, the Hungarian military's combat effectiveness, and even its mere functioning, have been called into question.[2] The political will to increase the defence budget in this case has been severely constrained by the state of the economy.

The psychological effect of defence cuts on the individual was further aggravated by the high rate of inflation throughout Central Europe. Rather than understanding that inflation in fact reduces the real effect of cuts in the defence budget, many simply saw the figures growing. The debate about reducing the defence budget touched a raw nerve because of its implications for employment in countries with a large military–industrial sector, such as Poland and the former Czechoslovakia.

Initially, inflation was the highest in Poland: 680% in 1990, 70.3% in 1991 and 43% in 1992. In 1990 in what was then Czechoslovakia, inflation ran at 65%. In Slovakia, it was 39.8% in 1992 and 12% in 1993. Even in Hungary, where the rate of inflation was relatively lower (35% in 1991 and 23% in 1992), the coincidence of the defence cuts and inflation led to a 60% decrease in the defence budget in real terms, while it increased nominally by about 57% in 1988–95.

Initially, defence cuts could almost be seen as a necessary side-effect of the reductions in manpower and equipment levels required by the Conventional Armed Forces in Europe (CFE) Treaty. Yet they continued. Ironically, the savings that could have been made proved

Figure 1: Real GDP Growth in Central Europe, 1989–1997

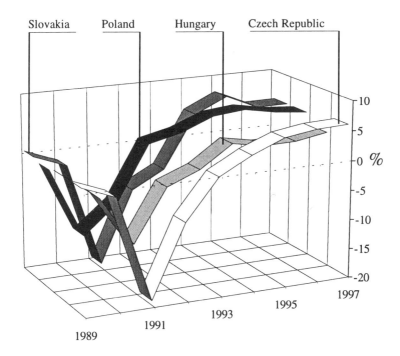

Notes: Figures for 1996 and 1997 are Organisation for Economic Cooperation and Development (OECD) projections.
Sources: International Monetary Fund (IMF), *International Financial Statistics* and *World Economic Outlook*; OECD, *Economic Outlook*.

negligible for the national economy. They were not sufficient to have a tangible 'guns-for-butter' effect and, moreover, the economic pay-offs were absorbed by the recession and the transformation to free markets. Not only did the defence cuts have no clear economic benefits, they actually increased costs in terms of reforming civil–military relations.

The Change in Regime, 1989–1990

Neither 1989 nor 1990 was the first year of *de facto* decline. Prior to 1989, increasing economic problems had caused a gradual but definite decline in military spending in all four Central European countries, but this was not made public. After 1990, however, defence expenditure was cut more sharply, and made public. Following the collapse of the Soviet

23

Figure 2: Decline in Hungary's Defence Budget, 1989–1995

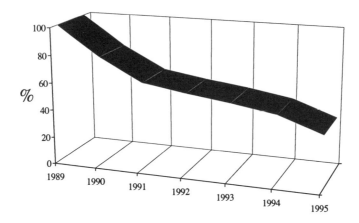

Source: Directorate of Management and Consultancy Services, UK Ministry of Defence, *Review of Parliamentary Oversight of the Hungarian Ministry of Defence and Democratic Control of the Hungarian Armed Forces*, D/MAN S (ORG)/60/Study 810 (London: Ministry of Defence, February 1996), p. 22.

empire, this decrease in the defence budget became just one of the factors threatening the military's financial status.

Severe and repeated defence cuts risk compounding the military's sense of being relegated to a 'minimum subsistence level' in the national budget, and ultimately enhancing their dissatisfaction with – and distance from – defence reforms including the introduction of civilian control. On the other hand, increasing the defence budget's share of GDP must be accompanied by government policies if it is to have a positive impact on civil–military relations.

Table 1: Defence Expenditure as a Percentage of GDP, Pre-1989

	1985	1987	1989
Hungary	3.6%	3.3%	2.8%
Czechoslovakia	4.7%	4.9%	3.7%
Poland	3.0%	2.5%	1.9%

Source: *The Military Balance* (London: IISS, various years).

Table 2: Defence Expenditure as a Percentage of GDP, 1989–1995

	1989	1990	1991	1992	1993	1994	1995
Czechoslovakia	6.8	3.6	2.6	–	–	–	–
Czech Republic	–	–	–	3.8	2.7	2.7	2.8
Slovakia	–	–	–	3.8	2.2	2.2	2.8
Hungary	6.3	2.0	2.1	2.2	2.3	1.8	1.4
Poland	8.0	5.4	4.6	2.3	2.6	2.4	2.5

Source: IISS, London.

Budget Priorities

In the mid-1980s, most of the Central European Warsaw Pact countries decided to decrease military investment substantially. Defence cuts were made at the expense of spending on research and development, and on military investment and were also absorbed by them prior to 1989. This had a particularly negative effect in Czechoslovakia and in Hungary.

While the defence cuts did not have an immediate impact on military personnel, they signalled the onset of the deterioration of military equipment that the new political elites were to inherit in 1989–90. By this time, the largest proportion of defence expenditure was spent on personnel and maintenance costs. As a result, further, post-1990 decreases in the defence budget were immediately and most directly felt by military personnel. It could be argued that the imbalance in defence expenditure has been the root cause of tensions since 1990 rather than the cuts in and of themselves. What the armed forces have to face in 1996 is the cumulative effect of a decade-old decline in the defence budget and, as important, its decade-old unbalanced structure.

Economic difficulties caused by the transition to market economies left the new political elites no alternative but to continue to prioritise manpower and operations and maintenance (O&M) at the expense of modernisation, investment, and research and development (R&D) while reducing the overall defence budget. Even in the few cases where investment marginally increased, little real modernisation or procurement has been undertaken. Statistics usually include the purchase of non-military equipment, as well as construction, under investment and development.[3]

Investment in the military has clearly been influenced by the policy goal of joining NATO. This was the motive behind the Czech decision to modernise its MiG-21 aircraft instead of purchasing Russian MiG-

25

29s. Similarly, it motivated Hungary in 1993 to replace its outdated airspace management-and-control system and to purchase the US Identification Friend–Foe (IFF) system – Hungary's only modernisation project since 1989.

Table 3: Defence Budgets by Function, 1995–1996

(%)	Personnel	O&M	Procurement	R&D	Infrastructure
1995					
Czech Republic	35	43	14	4	4
Hungary	52	36	8	0	4
Poland	63	22	12	2	1
Slovakia[a]					
1996					
Czech Republic	41	26	15	3	16
Hungary	50	35	9	0	6
Poland	69	15	14	1	1
Slovakia	40	32	20	2	6

Note: [a]1995 data for Slovakia are not available.
Source: IISS, London.

Public Attitude Towards Budget Cutting

Policy-makers in Central Europe often claim that public opinion is the primary force behind the defence budget cuts. Given the economic hardship the populace endures, even maintaining the defence budget, let alone increasing it, would lose the government popular support. Few empirical data are available to illustrate this, and no analogous data are available that would allow for a proper regional comparison. Yet what data are available shed doubt on the simplistic argument that public opinion is the primary driving force behind the defence budget.[4] Opinion polls in the Czech Republic and Hungary on the public's preference for increasing or decreasing defence spending do not show an unambiguous stance in favour of budget cutting. Moreover, the gap between the two opinions decreased from 17% in 1993 to 11% in 1994 as GDP grew.

A July 1996 poll by the US Information Agency (USIA) on the public's willingness to use state funds to upgrade their militaries to NATO standards shows a much bleaker picture: only 8% of Czechs, 9% of Hungarians and 7% of Slovaks were in favour of this. Of the 83% of Polish respondents in favour of NATO enlargement, only 23% were prepared to reduce other budget items for the same goal.[5] While these

26

views may reflect the long period of uncertainty about the future of NATO enlargement, Central European government policies have been clearly inadequate in outlining the costs of both NATO enlargement and of independent national defence. Despite the tough economic conditions in Central Europe, public opinion of whether to increase or decrease the defence budget is ambiguous at best.

'Military expenditures are a burden for the state' – Czech Republic		
	yes	no
1992	53%	41%
1993	55%	38%
1994	45%	34%

Source: *Democratic Control Over Security Policy and Armed Forces* (Prague: Institute of International Relations, 1995), p. 51.

'How much should government spend on the military?'– Hungary			
	less	same	more
1991	66%	22%	12%
1992	21%	20%	59%
1993	19%	22%	59%

Source: Ferenc Molnar, *A Magyar Honvedseg Civil Kontrolljanak Helyzete es Lehetosegei* (Budapest: Zrinyi Miklos Military Academy (ZMKA), 1996), p. 16.

Budgetary Challenges in Central Europe
Lack of Civilian Expertise
The conviction that civilian control of defence budgeting is essential for effective civilian oversight of the military has done little to develop civilian expertise in this field since 1990. Nor has this support been translated into actual cooperation with the West.

Parliaments have been fairly efficient in overseeing the implementation of the defence budget and the acquisition of military equipment. These are areas in which the level of civilian control of the military has been most successful. Parliamentary control of the military's budgetary requirements as presented by the Ministry of

Defence, however, is generally inefficient. While parliament checks the proposed budget's compliance with law, the relevance or effectiveness of the individual items are more often than not unchallenged. Much therefore needs to be accomplished in the planning and budgeting phases. Independent scrutiny of military requirements is lacking, and a network of external consultants and civilian experts – central to parliamentary control of defence in established democracies – must be introduced throughout Central Europe. If the lack of civilian expertise in defence budgeting continues to be chronic, the military will remain the unchallenged basis of decision-making. This, in turn, threatens to freeze the fundamental reform of civil–military relations in the mid-term.

The Structure of the Military Budget
The structure inherited from the pre-1989 defence budget has proved an impediment to reform. The Warsaw Pact's system of financing defence was designed to be impenetrable even for those who worked in it. It consisted of several independent budget 'circles' none of which contained the defence budget in its entirety. Some military expenditures and investments were not even accounted for as defence expenditure, but were included in the Finance Ministry's budget as quite unrelated to the military, for example under the heading of construction. Although the traditional five-year planning cycle existed, it was treated far more flexibly than the five-year plans in other areas.

In most of the countries examined, the presentation of the budget to parliament by the Ministries of Defence has barely changed since 1989 and remains poorly itemised. The budget's structure prevents its debate in parliament, let alone its modification, since it does not contain information in sufficient quantity or detail for parliamentary work. In Hungary, for instance, the document presented to parliament by the Ministry of Defence is sometimes only one page in length.[6] In addition, the parliamentary time allocated to discussing defence expenditure is inadequate.

The size of the defence budget is a particularly sensitive issue in Central Europe. Parliament's role is to ensure that defence spending and acquisition properly reflect the country's nationally accepted defence and security objectives throughout the budgetary process. That decisions concerning the overall figures, as well as the division of defence expenditure between personnel, equipment, maintenance and development, be the domain of the National Assemblies is of great importance for democratic civil–military relations.

Parliamentary approval of the defence budget does not in itself determine the budget items in most countries. Parliament's decision only binds the Ministry of Defence to the overall budgetary figures, thus leaving the Minister – and Ministry – of Defence significant discretionary powers.[7] In the Czech Republic, the introduction of the US Planning Programming and Budgeting System (PPBS), discussed more fully below, has begun to improve parliamentary insight into the defence budget . But the structure of the defence budget in Poland, Hungary and Slovakia still does not facilitate similar oversight and scrutiny.

The Legislative Versus the Executive?
Parliament's fiscal power to determine what fraction of national income is spent on defence is key for effective civil–military relations in all democracies. The armed forces always compete with other government expenditures for limited resources. The role of the legislative is to outline the basic principles of the defence budget in accordance with national priorities. But the executive, as the body that initiates and then implements the approved budget, cannot, or should not, exclude parliamentary scrutiny at later stages of the process.

In theory, parliament's role is pivotal in all aspects of defence expenditure, for example in basing its legality on parliamentary authorisation, and in ensuring that the money is spent as intended and in a cost-effective way. These powers mean that: all military funding is voted in by the legislative to ensure its compliance with national security-policy goals and other budgetary priorities; the legislative defines, or at least approves, the purposes for which funds may be allocated; and the estimates included in budget proposals are justified. This, in turn, necessitates investigating budgetary requirements and their proper accounting, and requires that military appropriations are made for a specified period. This latter power ensures that parliament regularly supervises national defence policy and revises it if need be. For the legislative's financial powers to be effective requires extensive legal and institutional support involving a whole network of budgetary supervision by final audit institutions and independent committees to alert the legislative to any malpractice, such as mismanagement of funds.

In reality, however, some of the above powers, or the means to exercise them, are not available to parliaments in Central Europe, if not for legal reasons then because of their practical limitations. In many cases, institutional and individual interests influence the reforms. In other cases, strict governmental fiscal policies force a one-to-one 'negotiation' between the ministers of finance and defence to determine the defence budget, ultimately reducing parliament's influence. Despite its role in determining the defence budget, the legislative has limited influence over the military, and most Security and/or Defence Committees face the greatest difficulties when they want to alter a particular item in the defence budget but leave the total figures the same. The 'executive independence' enjoyed in Central Europe is greater than that in most established democracies, leaving the fiscal powers of parliament more theoretical than practical.[8] Yet while these countries are in transition towards establishing and consolidating democratic institutions, the powers and responsibilities of their legislatives are far more important than those of legislatives in established democracies. Although effective fiscal power lies with the executive in all Central European countries, there is an overwhelming military presence in most of their Ministries of Defence. Therefore the executive's influence over decision-making at the expense of the legislative is not compensated by effective civilian control by the executive. Instead, in most of Central Europe military personnel develop the budget figures, estimate how much is needed and then implement the budget.

Adopting a Western Model
The PPBS Experience
The Czech Republic was the first Central European country to introduce an entirely new defence budget process, the US Planning Programming and Budgeting System.[9] This system, introduced in the US Department of Defense by Secretary of Defense Robert McNamara in the early 1960s, involved a complex set of procedures aimed at reducing inefficiency and duplication of weapons systems, and at improving the quality of defence spending. The new approach was intended to shift the budget's focus away from the traditional emphasis on personnel and facilities as inputs, to the outputs of military systems within the framework of a functional analysis of the defence budgets planned for one, five and ten years. Most US defence budget experts consider that PPBS has failed to achieve its main goals and has unnecessarily complicated the US budgetary procedure. Nevertheless, it was this system that the Czech government decided to adopt. The other Central European countries are also considering radical defence financial reforms. Slovakia has explicitly committed itself to introducing PPBS from January 1997, and Hungarian experts have also been investigating the system as an option.

The Initial Situation

In 1993, the Czech defence budget was in chaos. From the mid-1980s, it had been continuously decreasing and, as in the rest of the region, all investment projects had been halted and much equipment had fallen into disrepair. Although the categories of defence expenditure were known, no information was available on their objectives, the costs of different units, and so on. In the words of Deputy Defence Minister Kalousek, responsible for finance, the defence budget was 'one big budget goulash'.[10]

Obstacles to Introducing PPBS

On a practical level, there was much inertia towards introducing PPBS. The ideas on which the system is based had to be adopted, as well as new work methods, to start building up each unit and facility cost. The new way of planning the defence budget met far more resistance than was expected, and without the active involvement of personnel at every level of the military PPBS could not be introduced. Many of those involved saw the failure of any aspect of PPBS as an argument against the system as a whole. Members of the professional corps and the Ministry of Defence, however, who did believe in the US system, understood that it would lead to greater transparency, even though some also saw this as a threat to partial or institutional interests.

Changing the views of the military, of civilian policy-makers and of the public towards the military budget and, more generally, towards the army's economic problems, was one of the first problems encountered. Cutting national defence expenditures was a stated goal of the Czech government, but it was powerfully resisted by those on whom it was to have an impact. This made cuts across the board more politically feasible than cutting back on one specific item of defence expenditure.

On a more theoretical level, while PPBS involves long-term planning for a five- and ten-year span, the Czech Republic itself does not have a national budget plan that covers such a time span. It is somewhat pointless to commit the government to allocate a specific share of the national budget to defence without an approved outline for the overall budget. Planning military expenditure ten years in advance without an overall state budget framework is a concern to many national experts.

Successes...

The introduction of PPBS was promoted by civilian economists and budgeteers in the Czech Ministry of Defence. The defence budget was originally seen as the naturally monopolistic domain of military officers who had worked on it for many years. By creating an entirely new system, and one that required specialised knowledge, civilian experts put themselves on an equal basis with military financial experts, thus tilting the balance of influence over the defence budget away from the military towards the civilians. If for no other reason than this, PPBS has increased civilian oversight of financial matters. In its first two years, and despite the many difficulties it has faced, PPBS has already achieved many of its fundamental goals. Above all, introducing the system has enhanced fiscal transparency in domestic defence decision-making.

Unlike the military, members of parliament were generally in favour of budget cutting, believing that this was the only popular way to deal with defence issues. Little consideration was given to the impact of these budget cuts or to potential alternatives. PPBS, however, encouraged members of parliament to use the defence budget as a means of re-defining the country's defence forces in keeping with its new foreign and security policies. Promoters of PPBS in the Czech Ministry of Defence focused on convincing parliament to propose budget cuts on concrete projects, rather than on the overall defence budget.[11] This idea was initially greeted with enthusiasm, but parliamentary support subsequently subsided when it became clear that PPBS would require a significant change in mentality.

PPBS has encouraged a rational approach towards military spending. A prior understanding of national security goals, and not simply what the army needs, has now become the main factor in determining the defence budget. Those involved in its planning started by establishing national defence priorities and the resources necessary to fulfil them, not by determining what resources would be necessary to maintain the army's present structure. This is even more important since the state of the national economy imposes strict limits on defence spending which might increase the gap between needs and actual possibilities.

Domestically, PPBS has involved military commanders on practically all levels in economic thinking and in viewing their own activity not only from the point of view of military necessity, but also from that of financial cost. Externally, introducing PPBS has greatly enhanced Western understanding of the Czech Republic's defence planning process. By rendering its policies more transparent, it has also advanced the country's policy goal of joining Western security institutions.

... and Some Criticisms
Yet the introduction of PPBS was not the product of a comparison of alternative methods of defence budgeting. Ironically, many US experts had recommended that the Czech Ministry of Defence study other defence financing systems, such as the French or the British. Since the US experience of PPBS has itself been mixed, the concern that it may be too complex to export is legitimate.

PPBS is the only document legally binding on the Ministry of Defence. Its planning and programming aspects are treated exclusively as the Ministry's internal documents, and once the overall budget is approved by parliament, the Ministry retains the freedom to move funds around. Some personality issues have also tarnished the system's image. According to the intra-ministerial arrangements worked out by 1995, for instance, the same deputy defence minister was responsible for allocating funds as for controlling this allocation. PPBS has also been criticised for being too extreme: while it gives civilians in the Ministry of Defence effective influence over the defence budget, the military has been almost totally excluded from its development. More often than not, documents are being produced about the Czech defence forces without any participation by representatives of the military itself.[12]

The Czech Republic's defence reforms have not enhanced the role of the legislative. It continues to be easier by law for the Security and Defence Committee to increase or decrease the entire defence budget than to influence one particular project. If the Committee does not want to alter the overall budget but only to give priority to one project over another, it has practically no legal means to do so.[13] The introduction of PPBS has not been accompanied by the appearance of civilian consultants for the parliamentary committees. Thus, even in the Czech Republic, the most advanced of the Central European countries in reforming the defence budget process, civilian control has still not been achieved according to a Czech national expert.

Towards Western Financial Models
The other Central European countries are further behind in reforming their defence financial process. Their motives for, and the obstacles to, reform also differ. In Poland, for instance, the lack of civilian expertise has halted the reforms. In Hungary, the increasingly stringent economic conditions make any defence budget reform impossible.

In Slovakia, the country's decision to join NATO's Partnership for Peace (PFP) initiative motivated the introduction of reforms in this area.

In September 1994, it set up a new Department of Financial and Economic Forecasting to reform defence budgeting and programming, but not defence planning.[14] The Department's activities soon began to erode and its personnel was gradually moved to other departments. In November 1995, when the Ministry of Defence decided to introduce the US Planning Programming and Budgeting System, the Department was reinstated. Introducing the system in Slovakia was proposed by an external adviser to the Czech Ministry of Defence, and was motivated by similar political reasons as those in the Czech Republic.[15] The Slovak Ministry's *Directive Guidance* in this regard was issued on 31 March 1996, and gave January 1997 as the starting date both for PPBS and for the five-year budget planning phase. The document envisages that the system will be fully functional from 1998 onwards.

The Slovak Ministry of Defence's annual budget proposal is neither itemised nor specific. Even when the Ministry complies with an eventual parliamentary modification, it only has to do so in terms of the overall budget figures, not specific items, as in most other Central European countries. The Defence Committee has the right to request the Ministry to modify the budget, but that is the limit of its powers. However, to date the Committee has never recommended the slightest change in the defence budget.[16] While PPBS is being introduced, Slovakia is using the traditional Warsaw Pact budgeting system. This renders parliament's power to influence the military budget even more theoretical than in the other Central European countries.

There are signs of a transition to Western financial models in Hungary as well. Hungary's defence budget is regulated by laws approved by the new parliament after 1990, but these laws reflect the severe economic conditions of the time. The 1992 Law on State Financing together with the State Audit Law, the State Procurement Law and the Law on National Economy, provide the legal basis for the process. The national budget is prepared for one calendar year only, which limits developing longer-term defence plans. In Hungary, too, the lack of mid- and long-term planning for the national and defence budgets is a fundamental problem.

The Hungarian Ministry of Defence adopted the method of 'rolling planning' and programmed budgeting after 1990.[17] The planning cycle covers three years, with concrete commitment for one year only and an annual revision of the second- and third-year plans. The Ministry's defence budget has to be approved first by the National Defence Committee before being inspected and approved by the Budgetary

Committee. Proposals supported by both bodies are more likely to be approved by the legislative, although the Committees cannot guarantee approval. As in most other countries, parliament approves the total figures for the various items in the defence budget. Hungary's legislative has made serious efforts to restrict the Ministry's right to move funds around once the budget is approved: moving funds between sub-items within a main item requires the Minister of Defence's approval, but the details of the change have to be forwarded to the Ministry of Finance and the State Audit Office. If the proposed change involves moving money from one item to another, for instance from 'salaries' to 'material and equipment', it needs government approval. If the proposed change falls within the category of 'development', it requires parliamentary approval.[18]

The major problem for budgetary reform in Hungary is the division between the Ministry of Defence and the Home Defence Forces (HDF). While the Ministry follows a bottom-up process of establishing base requirements and tasks, the HDF and the General Staff – which coordinates the HDF's total requirement and its associate background institutions – follow a top-down approach.[19] The coordination between them inevitably leads to considerable tensions. The budget is supervised on four levels (HDF, Ministry of Defence, government and parliament), and each level tends to overbid for resources. The level of harmonisation between them is inefficient, and the higher up the supervisory ladder, the less efficient the supervision.

Conclusion: The Supervisory Process

While the law in Central Europe ensures parliamentary oversight of the defence budget, the structure of the budget prepared by the Ministries of Defence and the time-frame allowed for parliamentary debate are insufficient for effective civilian oversight. Decisions concerning the distribution of funding are usually controlled by the Ministry of Defence and the Ministry of Finance, but their responsibility does not extend to either the real necessity of the items or the efficient use of the allocated funds. The budget is accounted for and is subject to rigorous financial audit in most countries, but there is no assessment of 'value for money', nor are any alternative proposals developed for the budget items. In the successive stages of defence budget supervision, its effectiveness tends to decrease. Independent scrutiny of military requirements, a key mechanism of control, is lacking altogether in Central Europe.

Despite all legal arrangements to the contrary, the balance between the branches of government tilts away from the legislative and towards the executive in making the defence budget. The dominant presence of the military in the Ministries of Defence combined with their monopoly of insight into the fiscal aspects of defence renders civilian impact on the defence budget minimal within the executive as well. Budgetary item figures are proposed by members of the military, and are not seriously challenged by civilian policy-makers or budgeteers. Civilian influence at the first, planning stage of defence policy-making is superficial, non-effective, even non-existent. During the successive stages of defence budgeting, the Ministry of Defence retains the power to reallocate budget items. As a result, civilian and legislative control is minimised at all stages and is restricted to 'window-dressing'.

Parliament's fiscal powers are restricted by and large to delimiting the size of the defence budget. They are theoretical and retroactive at best. Effective fiscal powers are concentrated in the executive, and in the military personnel within the executive, in almost all Central European countries. Analysis of the factors influencing the defence budget in Central Europe demonstrates that political support for the military is as important for determining parliamentary allocation for defence as the economic and budgetary environment of the individual countries concerned.

III. REFORM WITHIN THE MILITARY

Reform within the military, and especially its professionalisation, is essential for effective civilian control in established democracies. Reforms that neglect the internal dynamics of the professional military are bound to fail in the long term. Restoring military prestige is also one of the four main criteria that define democratic civil–military relations.[1] In Central and Eastern Europe, restoring the military's prestige requires both the executive and the legislative to introduce a wide variety of policies, ranging from improving the system of remuneration and promotions to remodelling military training and education, and public relations. All these areas stress the importance of military professionalism in different ways and should help to create a positive public attitude towards the military.[2]

The Challenges Facing Reformers
Western Models and Concepts
The political convictions behind the civil–military reforms after 1989–90 were rooted in Western democratic values. The variety of Western models initially caused some confusion in Central Europe. Whether it was necessary to seek an individual national mechanism of civilian control, or whether it was possible just to adapt another country's model was one of the first issues discussed.

During the first five years of reform, all four Central European countries incorporated certain aspects or institutions from a variety of Western countries, adapting them to their individual national traditions. The Czech Republic, Hungary and Slovakia tend to prefer Anglo-Saxon models, while Poland tends towards the German system.[3] Dutch, Belgian, Swiss, Scandinavian and other models have barely been examined, despite the similarity in size and mission of these countries' armies to those of Central Europe.

Depoliticising the Militaries
Defence reforms pre-dated the first free elections in all four countries. At the end of 1989, the outgoing communist governments abolished political activity among the officer corps and dissolved the Communist Party's organisational cells in all three countries. In modern democracies, a large overlap between the officer corps and a particular political party is considered incompatible.[4] By the end of 1989, Poland's General Wojciech Jaruzelski had already abolished political education

within the armed forces, and began to replace some senior officers, although fears persisted that the hardliners would survive these reforms.[5] Hungary and the Czech Republic made similar changes, first by strictly limiting the Communist Party's activities within the military. At its 20 July 1989 meeting, the Hungarian Socialist Worker's Party (MSZMP) – the Hungarian Communist Party – dissolved its Committee on the People's Army and Party cells within the army. At the same time, personnel decisions were made without reference to Party considerations. In November 1989, 99% of the officer corps took a new oath on the Constitution of the Hungarian Republic (instead of the 'People's Republic').[6] Those unwilling to take the new oath left the army. In January 1990, political decisions and orders within the army were made illegal, and in March, parliament passed an act modifying the Constitution and the 1990 National Defence Act.[7] Under this legislation, the People's Army was re-named the Home Defence Forces, and the Constitution designated the Hungarian President as Commander-in Chief.

In Czechoslovakia, communist Minister of Defence Miroslav Vacek made Communist Party organisations within the military illegal in December 1989. In early 1990, he ordered all professional soldiers and conscripts to cease any political activity and to resign their membership of political parties. Only a few officers chose to keep their membership and to leave the army instead, while the overwhelming majority followed Vacek's order. In March 1990, the parliamentary Defence Committee approved a proposal prohibiting professional soldiers and policemen from joining trade unions. This became law in May 1991.

Yet these initial steps had to be carried much further in accordance with the new democratic ideals. Moreover, as some of the 'reform measures' had been developed by the communist governments, they needed major re-writing after the free elections to conform to democratic principles. Besides the political difficulties inherent in fundamentally reforming the military, this re-writing contributed to the military's impression that the reforms lacked unity and were contradictory. This increased the military's general discontent with the new political regime.

One of the measures introduced to depoliticise the military after the free elections, 'screening', or 'lustration' as it came to be called in Czechoslovakia, provoked particularly heated debate about its political desirability, its feasibility and the practicalities involved.[8] The screening process reviewed the professional qualities and political history of soldiers, paying special attention to their links with the previous internal military security and state intelligence services. This policy, however, risked creating more problems than it solved. While the new political elite in Czechoslovakia decided to carry out a thorough lustration process in the military, as will be discussed below, Poland and Hungary opted for a more cautious path. Interestingly, soon after the break-up of Czechoslovakia, Slovakia halted its lustration policy.

According to a study by the Institute of International Relations in Prague, the initial reason cited for personnel leaving the Czech military was the introduction of the new oath: 9,460, some 15% of the overall professional corps, had already left the service by September 1990.[9] The majority of these were under 30 years old.

Figure 3: Percentages of Personnel Leaving the Military

Retired *18.5%*

Dismissed *5.5%*

Refused to sign new oath *24%*

Left voluntarily *52%*

Note: The reason for dismissal was usually incompetence or poor physical condition.
Source: *Democratic Control Over Security Policy and Armed Forces*, p. 44.

The so-called 'Lustration Law' was enacted at the end of 1991 in Czechoslovakia, and everyone of the rank of colonel and above had to apply for a lustration certificate. Of the 7,125 officers who applied for the certificate, 18% (1,282) were found to have collaborated with the intelligence services. Among them, 61% were under 40 years old, and one-third under 30.[10] Practically all these officers had to leave the ranks. Among those dismissed in the first stage of lustration were 74 generals, 4,830 officers and 4,476 non-commissioned officers (NCOs).[11] There was, however, a way of avoiding screening and staying in the military – being appointed to a lower rank than colonel. This presented no problem for those who opted for it, because of their existing informal ties and connections. Indeed, many former political officers whose task had been to indoctrinate conscripts were simply transferred, for instance to become counsellors to the enlisted.

Screening, therefore, had some negative effects, albeit indirectly, especially on the structure of the Czech military. The lower and mid-level ranks were depleted as the younger generation of officers left, only to be refilled to a limited extent with those officers who had successfully avoided screening.

The positive effects of screening include its impact on the higher ranks. The number of generals decreased significantly from 240 in the Czechoslovak era to 20 by 1996, ten of whom had been promoted to this rank after 1989. One of the most visible changes this policy produced was in the composition of the General Staff. By 1996, not one pre-1989 member was still in place. Lustration was also carried out in Slovakia, but was halted soon after independence when creating a national military became the major concern. As political screening disappeared, the positions of the old military stalwarts strengthened. These 'old guard' retain their positions today, preventing the younger generation of military officers from advancing either in their positions or in introducing fundamental reforms.

While Poland and Hungary chose not to carry out such a profound screening process, they have also adopted conscious and concerted policies to create a younger military leadership. In Hungary, some of the senior generation of officers criticised these political changes, but not enough to represent a real threat to the new regime. Moreover, by the end of the first six months of the Antall government in 1990, only 44 of the 87 pre-1989 generals remained in their positions.[12] The maximum retirement age was set at 55, and a system of promotions was introduced to allow the younger generation to take over key positions more quickly. Although these steps were strongly criticised by some generals, the measures successfully helped to rejuvenate the officer corps. By the mid-term of Antall's government in 1992, the Army's reliability was not in question, nor did the KGB or hardline communists have any tangible influence over it. Many of these policies, however, were reversed after the 1994 electoral victory of the former Communist Party under Gyula Horn, bringing back many of the old military faces.

Increasing Military Professionalism
The Warsaw Pact system inhibited pure military professionalism and pride as well as the military's political neutrality, and loyalty to the Communist Party was a fundamental part of the military profession. Initially, the structure consisted of a web of incentives and disincentives, including material benefits, the possibility of social upward mobility, and promotions which largely depended on political loyalty. This system became less dominant by the mid-1980s as the military began to adopt

characteristics of political neutrality and professionalism. While the officer corps remained nominally servile to Moscow, it gradually became more and more politically disinterested as military professionalism increased. In this way, the military became a kind of hybrid institution 'loosely coupled' to the political system.[13]

In terms of the theory of civil–military relations, the goal of reforms after 1990 in all four Central European countries was to increase the Huntingtonian concept of 'objective military control', or to maximise military professionalism.[14] According to Samuel Huntington, this consists of expertise, corporateness and responsibility. In this concept, strategy is the domain of civilians, while the professional soldier needs freedom on an operational level. Whether separating the military totally from society is a necessary, let alone fundamental, prerequisite for military professionalism is debatable.[15] Professional members of the services as well as conscripts inevitably internalise civilian values by living among civilians for much of their lives. Such internalisation should be encouraged since adopting this value system ensures that the military never turns against its own society's ethics and norms. This is the essence of the concept of 'citizen soldier' as developed by Morris Janowitz.[16] Many experts claim that these fundamental approaches to the relations between military and civilian society are not really alternatives, but complement each other.

Practical policy-making in Central Europe since 1990 reflects this complementary approach. Increasing military professionalism in the Huntingtonian sense was discussed more publicly after 1989–90 and was expected to have several positive effects. If military professionalism means that the military incorporates the idea of civilian control, it becomes a solid foundation for democracy. Military professionalism was also expected to enhance military effectiveness and efficiency, thereby reducing the gap between Central European and Western military thinking. On the civilian side, the political goal of increasing military professionalisation led to a change in the mentality of many members of parliament from simply budget cutting to considering the implications of decreasing the defence budget. All the Central European countries are now set to increase their number of professional military personnel and decrease that of conscripts. In the Czech Republic, the document dealing with this issue goes as far as to call the future Czech army 'semi-professional'.[17] Yet the conscript system will be maintained at decreasing levels for the foreseeable future throughout Central Europe, if only to postpone the huge initial costs of switching to an all-volunteer army.

Despite the numerous positive effects of military professionalism, it is hard to prove that increasing professionalisation has reduced the military's indirect political involvement. Many experts in the region argue that if professional soldiers have become less inclined to be actively involved in politics since 1989, this cannot be primarily attributed to growing professionalism, but to political pressure by the new democratic political parties and by the press.[18] In any case, the idea needs more time to produce fundamental change.

Mutual Mistrust
The military as an institution is inherently resistant to change in any society. Defence reforms were hampered in Central Europe by the opposite political backgrounds of the military and the new political elites. Since the military personnel had inevitably been trained and educated under the Warsaw Pact system, the civilian elite detected political reasons behind the military's slowness in implementing the reforms. When their efforts to transform the military's attitudes and values, the 'deep structures', were thwarted, civilian distrust increased.

The military, for its part, felt under siege from many sides: from the new political elite, from society and the media, and even from those within its own ranks who supported the political changes. Many saw themselves faced with a growing sphere of civilians who sometimes lacked even the most basic knowledge of military affairs. They feared the army 'falling prey' to incompetent politicians and felt the need to prevent its degradation. Some openly expressed their concern and unwillingness to 'subject the military to a knife [of] people ignorant of military realities'.[19] The mutual distrust that characterised the relationship between the military and civilians in the three branches of government – in itself enough to undermine reforms – did not, however, affect the relationship between the military and the public at large.[20]

Downsizing, Restructuring, Redeployment and the New Mission
Reforming the military faced four major problems. After 1989, all Central European countries had to relocate their militaries since their previous deployment reflected the Warsaw Pact's strategic and tactical thinking. Redeployment involved significant costs, including not only the logistical and material costs of moving equipment and personnel, but also human costs. The difficulties moving represented for military families in terms of housing, schooling and work for spouses led many to leave the ranks.[21] The break-up of Czechoslovakia created extra difficulties for redeploying the newly formed Czech and Slovak armies:

while only 18% of all military units had been deployed on Slovak territory, almost all the military educational facilities were located there. One-third of all equipment had to be moved to Slovakia, and new educational facilities had to be opened in the Czech Republic.

The Central European militaries were also being restructured with an eye to compatibility with NATO military structures.[22] This meant changing from the division to the brigade system, while continuing to downsize as required by the CFE Treaty.[23] The guiding principle behind these structural changes was a move towards smaller and increasingly professional modern armies.

These structural changes were, however, exacerbated by several factors. The socio-psychological insecurity resulting from the change of regime put political pressure on the military. Economic and financial strains caused a sharp decline in the general welfare of the military, both the individual and the organisation. At the same time, the withdrawal of Soviet troops from Central Europe had serious economic and environmental consequences. The pains of economic transition imposed serious limits on relocation and restructuring, which in turn increased resentment among the ranks.

The fourth challenge facing the military was its post-Cold War missions. The new national foreign-policy goals in Central Europe and the end of East–West tension put further strain on the military's transformation. Since the prospect of major war significantly diminished after 1990, the military's so-called middle-range tasks, such as peacekeeping, peace-enforcement and humanitarian intervention – which involve a great number of non-military tasks – appeared on the agenda. The definitions of military success and military service are also undergoing radical change. There is a shift away from training for war towards training for the prevention of war, combining traditional soldiering with new concepts.[24] Training for 'operations other than war' – humanitarian, peacekeeping, peace-enforcement and observer missions – on such a large scale was new for Central Europe's militaries, public and even policy-makers.[25]

Over-sized militaries were part of the peace dividend in Central Europe. Militaries that had been trained for massive aggressive operations against Western militaries now had to adopt a defensive stance, build relations with their former enemies, and perform missions in many ways new for both Central European and Western militaries in the new cooperative international security environment. The newly independent Central European militaries have had to respond to international requirements while at the same time protecting their national interest. New training centres have been established in all four countries. Participation in international peacekeeping operations began to take a large chunk out of the military budget (for example, up to 5% of the Czech annual military budget).[26] But developing these new missions and international military cooperation had a tangible impact on civil–military relations in Central Europe, as the officer corps became regularly exposed to the functioning of Western militaries.

Reforming Military Education
Military education in the Warsaw Pact era focused on the study of war and produced primarily military historians, theorists of military strategy and operational art. Only a small part of academic training in national security matters involved grand strategy. If such grand strategy existed at all, it was highly militarised, and civilians were not trained in strategic studies at all. After 1989–90, training first had to be moved from Soviet and other Warsaw Pact academies back to national military academies. The numbers enrolling in military colleges have fallen dramatically since 1990, reflecting the poor public image of the military.

Education is a key way of changing the military's way of thinking, and for reforms to be effective, let alone initiated at all, it was important to decide under whose authority military education would fall. In the Czech Republic, military education has come to be considered an integral part of the national education system. In Hungary, the migration of responsibility for military education and equipment procedures from the military leadership to the Ministry of Defence was an important step towards increasing the government's influence.[27] In Poland, a Department of Military Education, under a civilian head but responsible to the Ministry of Defence, was formed in April 1990 by the Mazowieczki government as one of its first civil–military reforms. In 1993, however, under Minister of Defence retired Admiral Kolodziejczyk, the Department was ceded back to the General Staff. In Slovakia, military education remains under the General Staff's authority.

Major military educational reforms have already taken place in all four countries. In Slovakia, for instance, civilian universities are now offering courses for military personnel. Previously, the military educational system covered all necessary subjects from technical to social studies, and no officers attended civilian universities. For the first time in the country's history, military officers are now being trained in civil universities. Career soldiers have attended civilian university courses in subjects where it is impossible to obtain military education. In 1994, the Slovak Military Academy opened to civilians as well, with a somewhat altered curriculum.

At the same time, the role and function of existing military educational facilities is changing. Many have started to offer radically more language training. This is also a prime goal of Western cooperation. Although knowledge of common languages is very important for international cooperation, reforming the curriculum and including the education of civil–military relations should be a high priority for establishing democratic oversight of the military in Central Europe. Changing military attitudes can only start through education.[28]

A new trend can be clearly seen in the increased numbers of military personnel participating in educational at foreign military schools. Education at foreign military establishments has become practically part of the military education system in Central Europe. Data from Slovakia show that 35 military personnel in 1993, 72 in 1994 and 77 in 1995 took part in various exchange programmes in Western countries. In the Czech Republic, 324 military and civilian armed forces personnel had attended various courses – 273 short-term and 51 long-term – by January 1995.[29] On the other hand, there has been little focus on training civilians proper in these programmes, with some exceptions.

Fundamental reform of national military education is, however, lagging behind other civil–military reforms, with most measures yet to be taken. The gap in competence between civilians and military personnel still has to be shrunk. One way of doing so has been to increase familiarity with the experience of Western democracies. Yet reform cannot neglect training civilian specialists in national security affairs both at civilian universities and at military facilities. Reforming military education involves:

- civilianising both the teaching staff and the students of National Defence Colleges;
- enrolling more military personnel in civilian universities;
- providing courses in security and strategic studies in both military and civilian universities; and
- including in the curriculum the concept of civil–military relations, its problems and the practical and conceptual understanding of how to cooperate with governments.

The Officer Corps and Political Change

The New Role of the Military in a Democratic Society

Abolishing using the army to crush internal threats to the regime and increasing military professionalism were welcomed by the majority of the professional corps, as discussed above. The only legal ambiguity can be found in Slovakia. While its Constitution, in line with other Central European Constitutions, prohibits using the military to put down internal threats, its Military Doctrine continues to allow for it.

Banning the use of the military for economic activity, yet another communist practice, was also a popular step. The military's economic activities used to represent a notable portion of national economic production. From agriculture (harvest times), to industry, construction (including houses for local Party officials) and roadworks (leading to these Party houses), this work was often determined by relations between the local Party and military leaderships. Although difficult to assess the true extent, this work is estimated to have taken up 10,000,000 working hours of the Czechoslovak military's time in 1989, compared to 7,000–8,000 working hours per year and 2.5m kilometres of transport in 1970s Hungary. Non-military activities by the armed forces are forbidden in the Czech Republic (with the exception of military aid in case of natural disasters), and are very strictly regulated in the other countries. The military reacted very positively to these changes, perceiving them as increasing military efficiency and professionalism and contributing, if indirectly, to the military's new prestige.

Political and Economic Pressures

The most visible sign of the changing role of the military in societal priorities following the political reforms was the defence cuts, which challenged the military's formerly preponderant position in the financial sphere. Since 1990, many in the Central European armed forces have suffered from severe social instability, the negative public image of the military, its low social prestige as a result of policy-makers' mixed reactions towards it, and a sharp decline in individual welfare.

The cumulative effect of these factors have led to a massive outflow of personnel, a phenomenon often referred to as the 'bleeding of the ranks'. In the Czech Republic, the average salary of a young professional in the private sector is at least double that of a young military officer. This difference is even greater in Hungary, where 20% of officers and 45% of NCOs live below the minimum subsistence level.[30] Between 1993 and 1995, there were no statistics regarding the minimum subsistence level in Hungary. In 1995 however, an estimated 60% of the officer corps lived below the average wage.

The situation is somewhat better in Slovakia and Poland. There, budget cuts did not hit professional salaries as hard, and the military enjoys a higher social status. In the Czech Republic and Hungary, however, a large proportion of the officer corps realised that their economic welfare and social stability had deteriorated to a much lower level than that of their civilian peer groups. Political and financial insecurity among the military has been constant since 1989, and its cumulative effect has imposed additional strains on transforming civil–military relations.

Among the reasons for the large number of personnel leaving the armed forces are the poor personal financial situation, the lack of social appreciation, the lack of a promising career path, inadequate reward for the work involved, a pessimistic or tense atmosphere, the negative personal attitudes of the older generation of commanders, and the fact that skills learned can be adapted to civilian life, especially by those under 30. Many of this group who left the military in 1989 declared that they had originally chosen the career as a last resort because of their poor economic circumstances, and that they only needed to be given the opportunity to resign. On the other hand, many of the compensationary policies introduced in Central Europe have proved counter-productive by discouraging the older generation from leaving while encouraging the younger to do so.[31] Statistics also demonstrate that the financial situation of the majority of those who have left the military has improved and they generally feel better in civilian life.[32]

Both the decline of intra-military factors to retain professional personnel – such as salary and prestige – and the strengthening of extra-military factors – such as the new-found satisfaction of those who have left – attract members of the military to civilian professions. These factors also explain why certain members of the armed forces are more likely to leave the services than others.

Although this personnel outflow might seem to contribute to the success of the policy of downsizing, it was in fact a spontaneous phenomenon, undirected by policy. Among the first to leave were often the best and the brightest, with qualifications and knowledge that they could easily adapt to civilian life, and the young who had the most initiative. The fact that it was by and large one age group – those around 30 years old – who left the military led to an imbalance both in age and rank. The balance of personnel who remained in the armed forces tilted towards the older generation, many of whom had deeply ingrained

Warsaw Pact attitudes and in some cases were physically incapable of training conscripts fully. In terms of rank, the exodus further increased the percentage of high-ranking officers, leaving even fewer lower-ranking officers and NCOs. According to some Czech experts, this process deflated the lower ranks and inflated the higher ones.[33] This had a particularly negative impact on the structure of those militaries which had not been subject to lustration to any significant degree, but even in the Czech Republic, screening that targeted primarily the older generation of officers could not compensate for the negative effect of this spontaneous exodus from the lower ranks.

In Hungary, for instance, 60% of the company and platoon commanders who left the military were under 30 years of age. In the Czech Republic, some 28,000 professional soldiers, mainly young officers and NCOs, have left the armed forces since 1990, leaving 33.3% of the current total under 30 years of age and 66.7% above 30.[34] About 20,000 high-ranking and 10,000 middle- and low-ranking officers remain in the Czech Army.[35] Of these 0.1% are generals, 68.3% officers, 28.4% warrant officers and 3.2% NCOs. The ratios are similar in other Central European countries. Reversing this trend and increasing, in particular, the percentage of NCOs faces enormous difficulties in the current economic climate, and there is little realistic chance that the proposed strategies for personnel development can be implemented. Twenty-five percent of the professional corps were expected to be short-term, contract soldiers by 2005, a significant rise from 3% in 1996.[36] Financial difficulties are also delaying the recruitment of professional military personnel. A poll of conscripts in Hungary revealed that 23% would volunteer for service if military wages were higher.[37]

Good personnel policy is critical for effective civilian control of the military. Civilians in the legislative and the executive are legally entitled to devise a new military structure, establish criteria for promoting, commissioning, assigning and retiring officers, as well as make decisions related to military educational matters. However, without the necessary financial control this legal right remains purely theoretical.

Support for NATO Integration
Opinion polls demonstrate the military's consistently high level of support for NATO integration in all Central European countries. Support is by far the highest in Poland – well over 60% – where the officer corps adopted the national policy goal of NATO integration in a

very short period of time and with great enthusiasm. The percentage of Czech and Slovak officers supporting enlargement is also around 60%. In Czech opinion polls, 62% of military respondents were pro-NATO enlargement and 28% against.[38]

In Hungary in 1990–92, the majority of officers distrusted alliances in general, both the Warsaw Pact (68.7%) and NATO (64.8%), although 81.4% did believe in some kind of European security option and 39.8% promoted the idea of neutrality. These opinions soon began to change and in 1993 70% expressed pro-NATO views, and polls conducted every three months for four years show a consistent level of support of around 60% between 1992 and 1996.[39] Although this figure increased to 70% in 1993, it declined again to around 60% from 1994 onwards. This change is generally attributed to the effect of the war in the former Yugoslavia, but consistent and clearly expressed pro-NATO government policies also played a determining factor.

There are many reasons why the military supports NATO integration. NATO enlargement offers the armed forces a prominent role in the political transition process of their countries. It also promises social legitimacy and socially acceptable upward mobility both personally and professionally. The withdrawal of Soviet troops from Central Europe at the end of the Cold War was a major event for the independence of the national defence forces.

In most of Central Europe, the general population has a different attitude from the military towards NATO enlargement. In the 1993 Czech opinion poll, 62% of the military supported joining NATO compared to only 42% of the general public.[40] This latter figure increased to 56% following the visit of US President Bill Clinton to Prague. A poll conducted in 1996 among the higher-ranking military in Hungary indicate a significant decline in pro-NATO views in inverse proportion to the general population: 44% of the population, but only 38.5% the officer corps, favour NATO enlargement, while 42.2% of officers actually declared anti-NATO views compared to 35% of the general population.[41] As this poll focused on the higher-ranking military (58% of the respondents were senior officers, 38% officers and 4% NCOs), it may not be representative of the military as a whole. Yet it reveals one of the main consequences of the higher percentage of the older generation in the military. The figures also indicate a decline in the military's support for NATO integration from 1993–94, which questions the effectiveness of the Hungarian government's presentation of its NATO policies since 1994.

The Military and Political Participation Post-1989

Prior to 1989, Communist Party membership among the military was the highest of all other state institutions in Central Europe. Above a certain rank, Party membership was compulsory. In the Czechoslovak military, for example, all generals, 82% of officers and 51% of NCOs were Party members. Following the free elections in Central Europe, legal regulation of the officer corps' political involvement became a high priority, but no regulation could halt or even influence existing informal political–military connections. The officer corps' political allegiance after 1989–90 did not unanimously shift to one specific political party in any of the countries examined. This indicates that the high Communist Party membership among the officer corps, and definitely below certain ranks, was to some degree a superficial issue which did not reflect the real political conviction of the military in the Warsaw Pact era. Yet certain trends in the military's political attitudes are reminiscent of the Warsaw Pact.

Regulating the post-1990 political participation of the active military is an ambiguous process in almost all four countries. This ambiguity is most visible in Poland and the Czech Republic where the law prohibits the military's involvement in political activities in the barracks and membership of political parties, yet it permits serving soldiers to be nominated to party lists, both in municipal and parliamentary elections. If elected, military personnel only have to discontinue their active military duty for the period of their political mandate, after which they can return to their units. This legal regulation suggests that the military's political neutrality is fairly superficial.

While the law thus allows for some active parliamentary participation by the military, this has not occurred on a large scale in any Central European country. Only two military professionals served in the last Czechoslovak federal parliament in 1990–92, both as members of the Communist Party. In the 1992 general elections that led to the division of the country, 23 soldiers were on the list of candidates and most ran for left-wing parties. Of them, six officers were elected federal deputies, one for the Left Bloc in the Czech Republic and one for the Party of the Democratic Left in Slovakia.[42] The majority of these officers ran in Slovakia, reflecting the enhanced nationalist feeling there that ultimately led to the country's independence. The situation was similar in the 1994 local elections in the Czech Republic, and the few professional soldiers that ran for parliament did so mainly on left-wing party lists. In Poland, the 1991 election was the first test of the law, and it was passed positively according to many policy-makers.[43] At the 1993 *Sejm* and

Senate elections, however, more serving officers ran for parliament for various political parties.[44] The first signs that Minister of Defence Onyszkiewicz's order not to campaign at military installations had been violated was dealt with seriously and, by and large, it stopped.

Although the law permits the military to participate in politics with some restrictions, the military has had only a small *de facto* presence in all the post-communist parliaments in Central Europe. Yet this presence reveals the difference in outlook between the older generation of the military with their Cold War-type attitudes and the younger generation whose attitudes are much closer to those of their contemporary society.

Active participation in parliament may be the most visible sign of the military's involvement in politics in Central Europe, but it is certainly not the most important one. As part of the electorate with a valid vote, the officer corps exerts probably more influence on national politics than if it was actively involved in parliament. Although very little empirical research has been conducted in this field, the available data reveal some very interesting trends. The continued political sympathy of the military for the left was evident in the parliamentary debate on military involvement in politics in the newly independent Czech Republic. Here, the left-oriented parties criticised placing any limit on the political activity of the military, which they saw as a violation of human rights. The political centre and right, on the other hand, were concerned to minimise the military's sphere of political involvement.

The military's political orientation in Poland came to light during the 1995 presidential elections. Then President Walesa was known to have made significant concessions to the military's independence prior to the elections in an attempt to win military votes. Yet the election results show that in those electoral districts with a majority military electorate, former communist Kwasniewski gained significantly more votes than Walesa.

Empirical data collected in the Czech Republic reveal two parallel trends in 1996 regarding the military's political affiliation, divided along a generational line. It is mainly the older generation of officers who support, and are sometimes actively involved in, the left-wing political parties. While in 1990 and even in 1992 this was demonstrated by their willingness to vote for the Communist Party, as the reformed left-wing Party of Social Democracy (CSSD) grew stronger, it gained some of these Communist Party votes. Many of these military officers hold the post-1989 centre/right-oriented governments responsible for the decline in military prestige and standard of living. At the same time, political preference for other parties, primarily parties on the political right, increased mainly among the younger generation of professional soldiers. Their political affiliation is thus much closer to the general population's political preferences.

Table 4: 1996 General Elections Results in the Czech Republic

	left	*centre-left*	*centre*	*centre-right*	*right*
public	5.8%	12.2%	30.8%	25.8%	25.4%
military	9.1%	23.1%	49.0%	9.8%	9.1%
under 30	11.8%	13.7%	51.0%	13.7%	9.8%
over 30	7.6%	28.3%	47.8%	7.6%	8.7%

Source: *Agency Factum*, quoted by Marie Vlahova and Stefan Sarvas, 'Fostering Civil–Military Relations: The Case of the Czech Republic', paper delivered at a Joint SOWI–IUS Conference, Strausberg, Germany, 8–12 June 1996, pp. 24–25.

Combined, the votes of the military and the police for the left and centre-left show a similar discrepancy with the rest of the society (see below). Almost one-third of the military and the police together voted for extremist parties.

Table 5: Voting Patterns of the General Public, the Army and the Police

	centre-left	*left-wing*
	(Party of Social Democracy)	(Communist Party)
general public	26.4%	10.3%
army & police	38.0%	18.0%

Source: Research Department, Czech Ministry of Defence, Prague.

Empirical data thus clearly demonstrate the polarisation of the officer corps in Central European militaries, with the rift between the two generations widening and deepening. While no segment of the officer corps explicitly objects to civilian control, actual bureaucratic mechanisms and procedures continue in their traditional pre-1989 way. Many of the older generation's pre-1989 informal connections are unchallenged, and their sympathies towards the successor party(ies) of the former Communist Parties are alive and well. It is the older generation's deeply ingrained managerial habits and interests that influence the actual implementation of policies in most fields, including military education.[45] Even those among the older generation of the officer corps that do not have particularly negative attitudes towards the political changes prefer to stick to old practices and lack the dynamism and innovative zeal necessary for the new era.

The trends these developments indicate seem not to support the establishment of democratic civil–military relations or of a genuinely positive public image of the military in Central Europe. They are more likely to slow these down in the short term and, if they remain unchallenged, divert or fundamentally alter thorough transformation in the mid- and long term.

IV. THE MILITARY AND SOCIETY

Public Interest and Confidence in the Military: Regional Differences
Public support for the military is a prerequisite for stable civil–military relations in a democratic society.[1] This public support requires an understanding of the military and of its professional and social needs. The media, the government's own public-relations policies, academic writing, research institutes, NGOs and pressure groups all, in theory, play an important role in informing the public. However, in post-Warsaw Pact Central Europe, the media's role has tended to be more ambiguous and can become easily politicised, independent research institutes and NGOs are only nascent at best, pressure groups tend to focus on a single issue – mostly conscientious objection – and government public relations is in its infancy.

Little empirical research has been conducted on relations between the military and society at large. Overall, the public does not perceive the armed forces as a particular threat to the stability of the political system. Instead, they perceive it as under effective democratic control. While this public stance is broadly true for all Central European countries, their historic backgrounds and present-day relations are very different.

It is sometimes emphasised that the public image of the military in Poland and Hungary is at the higher end of the scale, while that of the Czech and Slovak militaries are at the lower end. There is a deep divide in the military tradition in Central Europe, as well as in the post-Cold War prestige of the military, but these do not follow the same lines.

Historically, Poland and Hungary have similar traditions. The Polish military tradition holds the rule of Marshal Jozef Pilsudksi in the interwar period in very high esteem, and the military is associated with a number of positive developments in nation-building and modernisation.[2] Although the rule of Hungary's Admiral Miklos Horthy during the same period had far less influence on the Hungarian military tradition, in both countries, the pre-1945 national military is remembered as having been on the side of national values, and as having actually fought several times for independence against outside oppression. The 1848 struggle for national independence against the Habsburg monarchy, which achieved major victories, is a great inspiration to the Hungarian military. In Poland, even General Jaruzelski's oppressive military regime did not destroy the public's historic esteem for the military. A large part of the Polish population still sees the Jaruzelski regime as the lesser evil compared to the Soviet invasion or the Warsaw Pact invasion that put down the *Solidarnosc* movement.

Unlike in Poland and Hungary, neither the Czech nor Slovak – nor the Czechoslovak – militaries have ever actually fought for national independence or to defend the country. The Czech Legions achieved considerable fame in France, Italy and Russia during the First World War, but did not fight on – or directly for – the Czech homelands. They continued to gain respect between the wars in their newly established country as well, but it was in the period shortly preceding and briefly following the 1938 Munich dictate that the Czech military enjoyed real national status. Despite the military's initial mobilisation, however, and its readiness to fight to defend national sovereignty, the political decision was made not to take up arms against Hitler's army.[3] This explains in part the Czech society's subsequent scepticism towards the military establishment.

The post-Cold War reality shows a different divide. The public image of the military in Hungary today is closer to the lower status of the Czech military than to the high esteem the Polish military continues to command. The Slovak military has reportedly enjoyed the high esteem of its society since its independence in 1993, which helped boost its image as one of the fundamental pillars of sovereign nationhood.[4] Contemporary statistics repeatedly confirm the high public esteem for the military since independence: 65% in March 1995, 70% in June 1995 and 72% in January 1996.[5] With a 70% level of public confidence, the military is the most trusted institution in Slovakia compared to others such as the police, the courts, trade unions or even the church.[6]

The terms 'public interest', 'prestige' and 'confidence' in the military are often used interchangeably, but there are important differences between them. Public interest does not include confidence in, let alone the prestige of, the military. Public confidence in the military has not automatically developed in parallel with public interest, indeed quite the contrary; as confidence increases, interest is likely to diminish.

In Hungary, a high level of public confidence in the military does not mean equally high prestige, as indicated by the falling numbers enrolling in military academies. Public trust and approval for the Slovak Army, which is seen as a major pillar of national defence, is very high, and pacifism is uncommon. A significant percentage of the Slovak public are also interested in foreign and security policies and in the Army's activities.[7] These notions are closely allied in Poland, mainly for historic reasons and, or perhaps despite, its political-military situation.

Of the four countries examined here, the army's image in the Czech Republic is probably the worst. Opinion polls have been conducted on a systematic basis, and show an interesting example of the de-linkage between public confidence in, interest in and the prestige of the military. By the time of the 1989 Velvet Revolution, the Czechoslovak Army was almost completely discredited in the public's eyes because of the officer corps' servility to the Communist Party and to Moscow. At this time, the public's interest in the military was also at its highest, but far from being a sign of respect or prestige, it was motivated primarily by fear of the military's involvement in the Revolution. As soon as the populace felt this threat begin to dissipate, their keen interest in the Army disappeared too. The Czech public's perception of the military became more positive after 1992–93 for several reasons. The government's lustration policies were welcomed by the public; the events of 1992 that led up to the separation of the state signalled a renewed sense of identity; and in 1993 the independent Czech Republic was created. In addition, the government's increasingly emphatic pro-NATO policy made the military seem a useful tool for Western integration. Of those polled, 38% in June 1991, 50% in May 1992 and 56% in October 1993 expressed confidence in the military. While these levels declined during 1994 to around 30%, data show a 57% level of confidence at the end of 1995.[8]

Public confidence in the Czech Army has thus increased significantly, while the prestige of the military as a profession has remained low. In a comparison of the popularity of 20 professions, that of army officer was ranked last but one in 1995, preceding only the job of cleaning personnel – and this despite the positive effect of the NATO enlargement process on the military's prestige.[9]

The electorate's political preferences have a noticeable impact on their confidence in the military, as extensive sociological studies carried out in the Czech Republic have proven. In 1990–92, public support for the military was expressed most strongly by left-wing voters (in late 1990, 56% of Communist Party supporters expressed their trust in the military). The general population at the same time had an interest, but no confidence, in the national officer corps. Polls in 1993–94 indicate a shift in the political background of those who trust the military to right-wing voters, 55% of whom expressed their trust compared to 49% of political centre voters and 42% of left-wing voters, a sharp decline from 1990. Thus two major shifts occurred in the Czech Republic since 1990: the general public's confidence in the military increased; and more specifically, it increased among voters of the centre and centre-right, while it decreased among voters of the left. Support for NATO enlargement also tends to follow the political divide in the Czech Republic.

Public confidence in the military changes depending on whether it focuses on the military as a threat to society, on its support for the democratic institutions created since 1990, or on the country's national goal of Western integration. As shown above, public confidence that the military poses no threat to society is solid in all four countries. Confidence in the other two aspects – its support for democratic institutions and the goal of Western integration – has attracted fewer studies.

The Czech public's positive perception of officers' attitudes towards democratic changes strengthened in 1991–93, from 24% to 33%. While public appreciation of the military's professional qualities is declining, the one aspect that has enjoyed a relatively consistent level of public approval is the military's support for democratic institutions. The military is thus not perceived as representing a threat to the functioning of democratic society.

Table 6: Public Views of the Czech Military

The military...	1991	1992	1992	1993	1994
...is well trained	59%	50%	50%	43%	39%
...has good morale and discipline	29%	18%	18%	21%	10%
...has the support of the public	46%	38%	38%	41%	22%
...is physically well prepared	57%	43%	43%	33%	24%
... supports democratic society	**24%**	**33%**	**33%**	**33%**	**22%**[a]

Note: [a]This relative decline is the result of a decrease in interest in military matters rather than a decrease in the belief that the military supports democracy.
Source: Democratic Control Over Security Policy and Armed Forces, p. 52.

Yet this relatively high level of public confidence decreases when it comes to the military's ability and willingness to support NATO enlargement. Public support for integration in NATO follows the political divide in the Czech Republic. A large majority of centre and centre-right voters are in favour of it, compared to those with a centre-left or left-wing political conviction who are not. Most important, expert studies have proved that these centre and centre-right voters tend not to trust the professional military's enthusiasm for NATO enlargement.

The Public's Attitude Towards Military Service

The public's attitude towards compulsory military service provides important feedback for the military, as it is through conscript service that the majority of the electorate form their view of the reforms already undertaken within the military.

In Slovakia, a survey of public attitudes towards the army's activities, public acceptance of these activities in their current form, and the relationship between the army and society, showed strong public support for joining NATO and criticism that insufficient information was available on European security institutions. The poll also revealed a slight discrepancy between public support for defence issues in theory and their readiness to participate in solving these problems actively. The public strongly believes that the army is necessary, yet it also believes that the army can be maintained without increasing the defence budget or improving conditions.[10]

Polls in 1993–94 in Hungary to estimate the impact of reforms in the conscript service has affected the public image of the military. The results show an almost equal distribution of opinions between those who thought that it had improved and those who perceived no significant change. In the fundamental reform of an institution so averse to change as the military, this is not a total failure.

Table 7: Hungarian Public Views on the Treatment of Conscripts, 1990–1994

	worsened	*unchanged*	*improved*	*don't know*
capital	6%	44%	30%	20%
major towns	5%	36%	45%	15%
countryside	15%	23%	40%	25%

Source: Hungarian Ministry of Defence, *A Honvédelem Négy Éve 1990–1994* (Budapest: Zrinyi Kiado, February 1994), p. 130.

An interesting facet of Czech public opinion is what some experts call the Czech popular *realpolitik*. Rooted in the performance of the Czech military in 1938 and 1968, and the policies of Western powers towards Czechoslovakia, this popular attitude claims that the Czech Army is ultimately redundant. The conviction that it is impossible to defend the country militarily, and that its fate has always, and continues to, depend ultimately on the will of the great powers, is strongly ingrained. This might also explain the relative decline of public trust in the military. This popular belief also holds that because of the historically low prestige and negative role of the Czech military, it does not and cannot attract innovative, successful people. According to this view, the Army is one of the most untransformable and old-fashioned of Czech institutions.

Table 8: Czech *Realpolitik*

	1992	1993	1994
'It is impossible to defend the country militarily'	62%	65%	48%[a]
'The country's fate is in the hands of major powers'	59%	58%	53%

Note: [a]This fall was accompanied by a sharp increase in those 'undecided'.
Source: Democratic Control Over Security Policy and Armed Forces, pp. 51–52.

Another important aspect of the public's attitude towards civil–military relations is its support for turning the national military into a professional army. In the Czech Republic, 56% of the general population would prefer an all-volunteer army, but this increases to 75% of those under 30 years old. As for the political and educational background of those who support such an army, they tend to be the right-oriented voters and those with higher education. Similar polls on the need for military service in Hungary indicated public support for military service in 1993–94: 81% said it was 'a patriotic duty', although 25% continued to call it a 'waste of time', and 41% a 'necessary evil'.[11] Yet when asked to choose between retaining the system of conscription and compulsory service or opting for a professional army, 51% favoured continued conscription while 47% chose an all-professional army.[12] In Poland, a similar poll revealed a generational divide: among the general population, 44.1% supported a future all-voluntary force, while 41.8% favoured retaining conscription. However only 18% were in favour of compulsory military service, with 66.4% favouring moving to an all-volunteer army.[13]

The Military and the Media
The military's relations with the media fall into two distinct categories: one that relates to the military media – that is, news produced and published by the Ministries of Defence for a military audience; and one that relates to the civilian media.

The military media is active throughout Central Europe. Prior to 1989, it was the military's propaganda machine, a communist 'public relations' department, and the military press was often more pro-communist than the Communist Party dailies themselves. Many of these newspapers continue to be written and read primarily by the military themselves. Some maintain the old tradition and reflect the Ministries of Defence's official position, proving just how slowly old practices change, and most remain under the supervision of the General Staff. Yet, after a few years of searching for a new identity, the military press has begun to change. It has tried to engage more qualified people to write, and some of the papers published by the Ministries have begun to express more independent and critical views. The most outstanding example is the case of the Hungarian *Honvéd* after the re-election of the former Communist Party in 1994. The paper's critical tone provoked hostility from the military establishment which threatened to sack the paper's editorial board should it continue to be so disapproving of the Ministry of Defence.

The appearance of military stories in the civilian media is a wholly new, post-1989 phenomenon. As such, it is only natural that it should create tension among the ranks previously used only to a propagandist, specialist press out of the public eye. It has taken the armed forces rather a long time to adjust to the new public interest in their activities all over Central Europe. There was relatively modest coverage of the armed forces immediately following the revolutions, even in Poland where the military has traditionally enjoyed popular interest and support. There, most post-1989 civilian journalists came from the political opposition to communism, and a large majority of them had never served in the military. As anti-communist activists against the Jaruzelski regime, they had refused military service and, after 1990, they lacked even the most basic military knowledge of an average conscript. A profound belief in pacifism was also part of the political credo of many journalists writing on military matters during the Cold War. Their dominant attitude towards the military was one of fear: in their experience, it meant threat and oppression.[14] In the Czech Republic, military journalists tended to come from the ranks of officers that had been discharged after 1968 for political reasons.

What began to change the relatively sparse coverage of the military in the region was a growing interest in NATO cooperation and enlargement. Gradually, this expanded to include issues relating to civil–military relations. The free press has been criticised by the military practically throughout Central Europe. Charges levelled against it have included the journalists' inexperience in military matters, their lack of insight and their lack of depth. In all four countries the military raised similar objections: the media only wanted scandals, not proper news; to the media only bad news is good news; and that publishing negative stories about the military had a negative impact on its attempt to create a positive new public image for itself. Some military officers went as far as to say that the media had contributed directly to the deterioration of the military's public image. The media's approach caused many of the top military leadership to become defensive and attempt to reduce the outflow of public information. This in turn provoked further media criticism. Given the paucity of domestic sources of information, journalists began to turn to foreign sources. The lack of clear guidelines regarding the classification of material in the Czech Republic further aggravated the situation. On most occasions, journalists had to wait for a Ministry of Defence official to decide how to handle the requested information. In Hungary, on the other hand, the media has sometimes proved a last-resort source of pressure for the legislative in trying to obtain information from the Ministry of Defence or from the General Staff. Media coverage can often be politicised, and it has been observed that in the Czech Republic the tone depends very much on an individual press organ's relationship to the government in power.[15] In Slovakia, the media, and especially electronic media, are almost entirely under governmental control, and this is reflected in the information conveyed.

In Poland, relations between the military and the media were, and to some extent continue to be, the tensest in the region. There, as media representatives would put it, the military's intrusion into politics gave the press the initial impetus for their coverage. In 1994, the first major media story concerning the military was the so-called 'Drawsko Affair'. At this infamous dinner, top military leaders had apparently openly criticised then Minister of Defence Admiral Pjotr Kolodziejczyk, allegedly on the President's initiative. The media accused the military, and specifically the Chief of the General Staff, of wanting to dispense with civilian control, which led to a swift counter-attack by the General Staff, who accused journalists of lacking professionalism and knowledge of military affairs. The General Staff claimed that while the public at large supported the military, the media's criticism revealed a lack of patriotism among journalists who 'are not Poles, not patriots'.[16] The 'media versus the military' affair thus became the 'media versus the military and the nation'. Polls of the officer corps give further proof of this peculiar media versus military war in Poland. An overwhelming 60% of the professional military felt that the civil media had a negative influence on the military's image, while 27% felt the opposite. When asked about the media's reporting of conditions for conscripts, the professional military's view was even more negative: 77% believed the media was overly critical, and only 16% detected positive reporting.[17]

Most Ministries of Defence have, however, begun to implement positive media policies, despite the difficulties described above. One of their first moves was to establish Public Relations or Information Offices to handle press relations. These offices have been organising meetings, round-table discussions, providing official information, and even allowing the media to observe army manoeuvres. In the Czech Republic, similar offices have been established at military headquarters, army corps and some brigades. Their primary goal is to improve communication with the local population and authorities. Sometimes an officer is tasked specifically to work with the press, otherwise the commander himself is in charge. The Czech Ministry of Defence organises specific courses for journalists in military affairs, as well as for those reporting on the war in Chechnya or the former Yugoslavia.[18] In order to improve the situation in Hungary, the Ministry of Defence launched a so-called Correspondent's Club in 1995, which today has some 85 members.[19]

The Ministries of Defence have also started to analyse the contents of press reports about the military in Central Europe. While it is impossible to provide a standard measure of a 'positive' or a 'negative' article, Ministry of Defence statistics indicate the general climate in Central Europe. The press review prepared by the Czech Ministry's Information Office, for instance, showed that 12% of all press coverage of the military was negative in 1991, and 6% in 1992.[20] Available data from Slovakia are far more neutral. In 1995, when the research started, it was conducted on a monthly basis. The percentage of negative articles, according to official Slovak reports, was 4–11%, the percentage of positive ones 3–15% and that of neutral ones 78–91%.[21] These numbers may indicate either the tepid interest of the Slovak media in defence matters, their lack of information, or the Ministry's generous definition of the terminology. In Poland, some 170 articles in more than 30 dailies and journals were analysed in 1994–95. These concluded that apart from the military dailies, only an insignificant number of civilian papers handled any military-related issue neutrally, let alone positively.

Clearly, far more effort needs to be made if the military is to understand the role of freedom of speech and the civil media's interests. The understanding that the civilian media cannot be expected to represent the interests of the military or to be its mouthpiece has to go hand in hand with the understanding that the media contributes to the democratic process through being at once critical and supportive of the defence establishment. But to be effective the media needs to have as much information as possible from domestic sources, within the limits of national security. The military tends only to provide positive information and to delay giving out negative information.

The post-1990 reforms of civil–military relations cannot be considered without appreciating the role of the media. The increase in the military's political neutrality cannot be solely attributed to the success of legal reforms, and even less to the mixed results of reforms within the executive or in institutional transformations, but has been greatly aided by the consistent, and continuously increasing, pressure of the media. The executive and the legislative have made limited policy efforts to create a positive public image for the military and to improve public understanding of defence issues, including NATO enlargement. But it is the media that have played the most active role in this process in most countries in Central Europe.

V. THE ROLE OF WESTERN POLICIES

Western Interest in Central European Civil–Military Relations
Western policy-makers developed an interest in civil–military relations in Central Europe after the break-up of the Warsaw Pact for several reasons. Primarily, they needed to determine how the Soviet-trained officer corps would react to the political changes in Central Europe, and whether they represented any challenge to democratisation. The level of civilian involvement in security and defence policy-making is an important indicator of the stability and democratisation of the consolidating democracies of Central Europe. The survival of the Warsaw Pact political and military mentality among the officer corps was perceived as a major risk by both Western and Central European policy-makers. As a result, supporting the democratisation process through, among other policies, establishing democratic civil–military relations in Central and Eastern Europe has been high on the agenda of Western democracies since 1989–90. Western policies since 1990 fall into two distinct categories: pre- and post-Partnership for Peace.

The Pre-Partnership For Peace Phase
The initial phase of interest in Central European civil–military relations centred on Western political support for democratisation. By placing special emphasis on civil–military relations, the West's civil–military policies were oriented primarily towards the military, a stance favoured by the Central Europeans. The military's reaction was a similar concern for the stability of political reforms.

NATO's 1991 *Strategic Concept* was the first key document to promote active cooperation with Central and Eastern Europe. This new document included two existing concepts of defence and dialogue, and adopted a new one: cooperation with countries to NATO's east. The document also emphasised the role of shared democratic principles by East and West. As establishing democratic civil–military relations was one of these newly shared values, NATO began actively promoting it. This principle gradually became one of the fundamentals on which NATO's relations with Central Europe were based. At the same time, it also promised to influence the actual roots of defence policy-making rather than dealing simply with its 'symptoms', the resulting policies. The document specifically recommended developing practical ways of implementing civilian control of the military. The US introduced four practical measures after 1991: the International Military Education and Training (IMET) programme and the Cooperative Threat Reduction (CTR) programme in 1991; the Joint Contact Team Program (JCTP) in 1992; and the George C. Marshall European Center for Security Studies in 1993.

The priority for Central European policy-makers in the initial stage of reform was to establish the democratic institutions of civilian control in their countries. Their policies were driven by Western ideas and models from the very beginnings of the transition process. Central European policy-makers studied the various Western institutions and many were established in Central Europe, adapted to national peculiarities and traditions.[1]

The emphasis on the individual rights of soldiers, on leadership and the civic education of the armed forces, as embodied in the German concept of *Innere Führung*, was carefully studied throughout the region and adopted in most countries, as was the post of parliamentary speaker for soldiers' rights, the *Wehrbeauftragter*. The strong civilian administrative component in the UK Ministry of Defence was also closely examined. The fact that only the very top-level leadership in the Ministry changes when a new government is elected in London is very different from the radical personnel changes following government changes in many other Western countries. As discussed in Chapter II, the US Planning, Programming and Budgeting System – which clearly defines the central relationship between the executive and the legislative and forces decision-makers to plan several years ahead, calculating cost and benefits and introducing a rational approach to defence financing – was most closely studied in the Czech Republic. The division of political tasks and authority between the President, Prime Minister and Ministry of Defence, according to the Constitution and law, was inspired by the French *cohabitation*. Spain and Portugal's radical transformation of the relationship between the executive and the military high command in their transition to democracy was not, however, studied as closely at first as perhaps it could have been. But its relevance to Central Europe's transformation gradually became apparent in establishing a balance between professional efficiency and democratic values in defence. The experience of smaller and medium-sized countries, such as Belgium, the Netherlands and Denmark, and of former neutral countries, such as Austria and Finland, could have offered more relevant examples. These, however, have not been examined as closely as would have been useful.

The Partnership For Peace Phase

In 1993–94, two phenomena began to characterise relations between Western countries and Central Europe. At this time, Western interest and cooperation in civil–military relations underwent both a quantitative and a qualitative change:

• *Increase in volume:* The amount of interaction between the two sides greatly increased as PFP gave new impetus for practical day-to-day cooperation between NATO and Partner countries. The increase in contacts and common projects between NATO and the Central European states was even more marked when compared to the North Atlantic Cooperation Council (NACC). Many initiatives were undertaken to promote civil–military relations in Central and Eastern Europe in the spirit of PFP, both bilaterally and multilaterally. Most NATO member-states organised programmes to introduce their national systems to their Central and Eastern European counterparts. In addition, the Allied countries began individually promoting the principle of civil–military relations in their own national tradition and Constitution. NATO's decision-making process also offered a good working example of civilian control of the military. NATO as an institution also initiated several programmes with special emphasis on civil–military relations, together with other organisations such as the North Atlantic Assembly, universities and research institutions, which organised seminars and workshops on various practical issues, such as accountability and defence budgeting. Thus NATO began increasing its information activities to help establish and consolidate democratic civil–military relations in Central Eastern European countries.

• *From support for democratisation to criteria for enlargement:* At the same time, civil–military relations gained a new significance in the West. Since 1990, the security dilemmas of Central and Eastern Europe have provoked increasing discussion of the future role of NATO.[2] During 1994, civil–military relations came to be seen as a fundamental requirement for NATO enlargement, partially in response to Central Europe's request for the criteria to be clarified. While civil–military relations were among the main requirements for membership, there was little common understanding of the principle among the NATO countries themselves. The fundamental principle of civilian control of the military is understood in a similar way by Western countries, but its actual implementation differs widely. From 1993–94 onwards, NATO, the European Union and the Western European Union (WEU) also referred to the criteria of membership in these organisations. In the course of

1994–95, effective democratic control of the military became a fundamental requirement for NATO enlargement.

The most often cited definition of civilian control of the military is that by Jeffrey Simon, published in 1995.[3] The basic principles are:

- clear division of authority in Constitution and/or in law;
- parliament's role in controlling the defence budget and deploying armed forces in times of emergency and war;
- restoring military prestige; and
- clarifying the role of civilian Ministries of Defence.

PFP encouraged democratic standards in defence policy-making within NATO itself by establishing working contacts among officers and soldiers of NATO member-states and Partner countries. Prominent among the objectives of PFP are practically all aspects of democratic civil–military relations:

- facilitating transparency in the national defence planning and budgeting processes;
- establishing enduring democratic control of armed forces;
- clear legal and Constitutional frameworks;
- chain of command from the military to government through a civilian Minister of Defence;
- qualified civilians working with the military on defence policy, requirements and budget;
- a clear division of professional responsibility between civilian and military personnel; and
- effective oversight and scrutiny by parliament.

In practice, however, PFP continues to emphasise military participation, and the actual shift towards involving more civilians has been marginal. The areas that are treated as priorities are military and technical: command, control and communications systems; standard-isation; defence infrastructure; logistic planning; military education; exercises and training. The few token civilians who participate in some of these programmes only give the illusion of change in both NATO and Partner countries.

PFP has also encouraged some Partner countries to take democratic standards in defence seriously by increasing transparency in defence planning and budgeting, thus facilitating democratic control of the armed forces. In their individual 'Presentation Documents', all countries undertake to cooperate in achieving transparency in defence planning and to ensure or strengthen democratic control of their armed forces. In this sense, PFP has already set the trend for civil–military relations in Central Europe, and successive NATO documents continue to emphasise its importance. Practically no NATO paper can appear without mentioning civil–military relations.

The 1994 *National Security Strategy of Engagement and Enlargement* is perhaps the most important official document to outline the new significance of civil–military relations.[4] On the criteria for candidate countries to join, the *Strategy* mentions 'appropriate' civilian control of the armed forces. The use of this term indicates the complexity of civilian control, and the phrase 'stabilised, or irreversible process of civilian control' has been recommended by many Central European politicians instead.[5] Overall, both the intensity of the programmes and the political importance of civil–military relations fundamentally changed in 1993–94.

Western Policies in Favour of the Military
Western initiatives before and after PFP have all tended to involve a large majority of military personnel. Partnership for Peace was not specifically designed to improve civilian control of the military. From its inception, it had an excessive military-to-military focus. In the early stages, it was even called 'the NACC for soldiers', which, from the point of view of establishing democratic civil–military relations, risked being a step backwards.[6] If PFP does have a positive effect on establishing democratic civilian control of the military in Central and Eastern Europe, this is a 'positive side effect' of the programme, particularly in those countries that treat PFP as a stepping-stone for joining NATO.

Extensive military-to-military programmes were set up on both bilateral and multilateral bases, for strategic as well as political training. Military-to-military programmes, however, still have no 'civilian-to-civilian' counterparts. At consultations, exchange programmes, courses or seminars, a large majority of Central European participants have been, and continue to be, representatives of the military. This is not to say that there were no civilian participants or projects designed for them in the PFP programme, but that their involvement has been nominal.

An essential part of the PFP programmes continues to be military exercises, and training and exercises for joint peacekeeping became one of the major pillars of PFP. Yet even educational programmes that offer courses in strategic studies attract mainly military personnel, with some token civilians. The programmes civilians most often participate in are language courses which do not cover security issues or strategic studies, let alone resource management. Civilians who attend these courses are selected largely because they are language teachers. In 1991 the IMET programme was expanded, and although it 'strongly encouraged' training civilians, this was not made a mandated requirement.[7] According to the military from all four countries, uniformed people have far more opportunities to participate in Western educational programmes than civilians.

Little statistical research has been conducted on this. Educated estimates are available from Central European Ministries of Defence, which put the ratio of military to civilians in Western programmes at 90 to 10. The situation is similar throughout the region. For example, some 35 Slovaks took part in different Western programmes in 1993, 72 in 1994 and 77 in 1995. Their ranks ranged from captain to colonel to brigade commander. Six Slovaks each year attend a course at the Marshal Center in Germany, 6–10 attend courses in the US, a similar number in France, and four in Hamburg. Of these, 90% are military personnel, and only 10% civilians.

Reasons for the military's almost exclusive participation in these courses include the West's concern to involve more military personnel in exchange programmes. Informal ties among Ministry of Defence staff have also influenced the selection of participants to these programmes. In some cases, Western training was used as a 'fill-in' for those who were temporarily without work or position in their home Ministry. As few members of Central European militaries speak Western languages, only a relatively small circle is involved in the programmes. A new culture developed out of these so-called 'travelling ambassadors' who travel from one exchange programme or training to another. Others who lack either sufficient language skills or the necessary connections never have the chance to participate.

This is not to deny the beneficial aspects of these programmes for overall civil–military relations: not only have these contacts contributed to a better understanding between Western and Eastern militaries, but Central European military personnel often returned from these programmes with a new mentality about the role of the media in defence issues, or that of civil–military relations in general. Promoting graduates of these NATO courses to higher positions in the army has visibly enhanced cooperation between the military and the media, and many have stopped perceiving the media as the enemy. International exercises have also had a positive impact on the military by changing their opinion of many practical aspects related to civil–military relations, such as the relationship of Western militaries to their civilian leadership or the attitudes of and interaction between these militaries. Joint training exercises and working contacts have greatly increased the Central European military's exposure to Western thinking.

Nor have civilians been discriminated against. The focus on the military in this first phase of cooperation between NATO countries and Central and Eastern European countries was essential in 1990 and was given priority for legitimate reasons. There seemed to be an almost unspoken division of labour between NATO countries and Central European governments: the West focused on the Central European military; while Central European policy-makers focused on the legal and institutional aspects of establishing civilian control. Yet, since then, the election of a variety of new governments in Central Europe has placed an added burden on testing the effectiveness of the West's initial focus on the Central European military. Indeed the commitment of these new governments to establishing civilian control of the military is a matter of great concern, as will be discussed in the next chapter.

Despite some beneficial aspects, the overall impact of the programmes for establishing democratic civil–military relations has been far from unequivocally positive. What is required is not exclusive civilian influence over defence issues at the expense of the military. Instead, expert knowledge by both civilians and the military must be recognised as mutually beneficial and necessary. The continued lack of a balance between the military and civilians risks having serious repercussions for the long-term development of democratic civil–military relations.

The Repercussions of Western Policies
The Loss of Civilian Comparative Advantage
In 1989–90, the new political elite suffered many handicaps in their attempt to establish civilian oversight and re-orient their countries' foreign and security policies, among them the lack of specialist knowledge of military and security affairs, of neutral and efficient administrative structures, and of expert advice. The one advantage they did enjoy over the military was their significantly greater exposure to democratic principles and practices prior to 1989. Knowledge of

Western political thinking, practice and connections were important assets in their attempt to gain acceptance and genuine respect in the eyes of the military.

The military's greater exposure to Western thinking, as a result of Western policies since 1990, should offer a perfect foundation for effective cooperation between civilians and the military. Yet civilian expertise in defence and military matters is still lacking and no programmes have been created to increase it. As a result, civilians are losing the comparative advantage they enjoyed before 1990. Instead of closing the gap between civilians and the military, the expertise gap is deepening and consolidating.

The Military's Criticism of Civilians is Justified
The lack of civilian expertise in defence matters is further aggravated by the military's growing security expertise and knowledge of Western political issues and practices. The military's contempt for incompetent civilian leadership has a precedent in the US Civil War phenomenon of what has been called 'Upton's Disease': the expert military loses confidence in the factually incompetent civilians and wants to save itself from them.[8] This 'disease' has characterised Central Europe since the initial reforms in 1989–90.

Western educational and training schemes have had a beneficial impact on the military's acceptance of Western democratic concepts. Yet without being balanced by similar civilian training programmes, they have added to the military's disregard of, and distaste for, civilian policy-makers in Central Europe. The strengthening of the military's poor opinion of civilians has been an unintended outcome of Western policies, but it risks ultimately excluding civilian authorities from military affairs.

The Gap Between Theory and Reality
Another handicap caused by the lack of civilian expertise is that the military's theoretical understanding of civilian control could not be accompanied by its practical implementation. Thus, the gap between theory and reality has remained constant or has even increased. Rather than political or theoretical obstacles, the impediment to appointing civilians in the Ministries of Defence, or for those appointed to be influential, has in many cases been practical in Central Europe. As the lack of civilian experts and thus the gap between reality and principle become chronic, it will most likely slowly but steadily corrode the

concept of civilian control in the eyes of the military. If the democratic principle is undermined, there is little chance that, despite a thin layer of official declarations, defence will in essence shift to the civilian sphere.

Control as the Domain of the Military

Above all, there are indications that, ironically, Western exchange programmes have not succeeded in their primary goal of altering the military mind as it was hoped they would.[9] The military has no interest and no reason to defer to the civilian sphere. Moreover, it has most of the necessary means to pursue its interests actively. The older generation of officers has no particular interest in ceding its positions to civilians or to more progressive-thinking colleagues, let alone in promoting civilian acquisition of military knowledge. These officers also influence media access to information about the military, and are likely to present to the public a minimalist, positive view of civilian control of the military. Yet some of the younger generation of the military genuinely believe in the principle of civilian control. In Slovakia, for example, the younger officers actively promote it. In Hungary, two years after the 'remilitarisation' of the Ministry of Defence, the situation is even more ironic: there, the older generation of the military has taken over the more powerful positions in the Ministry and is thus in charge of establishing civilian control.

The civilian sphere can by and large only pursue a retroactive, follow-up policy, to military initiatives, not a pro-active one: civilians cannot challenge the military's attitudes at any level, nor can they develop alternative policies. Military concepts are not seriously challenged at any level and no alternatives are developed. Instead, civilian oversight can only be exercised in bits and pieces, here and there. Current practice in Central Europe shows a more superficial acceptance of democratic practices than a real one. Legal control may be in the hands of civilians, but effective control depends on the advisers and close associates of the top-ranking leadership in the Ministries of Defence: largely military personnel. In these circumstances, civilian oversight of the military is becoming a 'virtual oversight'.

These problems are even more striking when comparing the post-1989 transformation of Central Europe to that of Germany after the Second World War.[10] The German Army had to undergo a process of dual integration: both integrating the soldier into German democracy; and integrating Germany into the Atlantic Alliance. Integrating the German military into a democratic, functioning society was a major policy issue between 1950 and 1955. Its primary focus was civilian: a large number of civilians from different churches, labour unions and youth organisations attended courses in American and other universities to discuss what kind of soldiers Germans wanted in their army, the role of parliament in the democratic oversight of the military, and other issues related to establishing democratic civilian oversight of the military. Nothing like this has even come close to being adopted in Central Europe, although the tasks faced there are no less momentous.

CONCLUSION: THE RISK OF FORFEITING REFORMS

It is impossible to understand fully the intricacies involved in reforming civilian control of the military in Central Europe without examining the broader political context. Following 1989–90, two fundamentally new security-policy goals were introduced in all four countries: reforming the defence establishment and introducing democratic civilian oversight of the military; and re-orienting foreign and security policies to aid integration into Western security structures. These two policy goals are not alternatives, nor is one more important than the other. Instead, they should be mutually reinforcing. Without a new, sovereign and democratic chain of command, no independent national security policy can be successful.

After the fall of the Berlin Wall, the priority of all political actors in Central Europe was to transform the military; depoliticise the officer corps; break the military's links with the former communist parties; subordinate the armed forces to state institutions; improve the conditions of those in military service; and increase military professionalism. Although in 1989–90 Soviet forces were still in Central Europe and NATO integration was far from a national policy goal, the domestic policy goal of establishing democratic control over the military was a priority.[1]

The clear vision and intention of the new Central European governments came from their pre-1989 opposition to the communist regimes and their commitment to democratic values. For example, *Charta 77* had already mentioned the need for civilian control of the military. The new political elites were also well aware of the potential threat of the military's involvement in the political transition. This threat was most immediate in the then Czechoslovakia, where the military leadership voiced its readiness to 'defend the achievements of socialism' and proposed concrete measures to crush the demonstrators.[2] In Poland, the main worry was Russia's direct influence over the military, and the new political leadership in Hungary also expressed this concern.[3]

The new Central European political elites thus did not consider the two security policy goals as linked in any way, but as independent and equally important aspects of the new democracies. New decision-making channels in security policy and a new chain of command and authority over the military were, at the same time, domestic prerequisites for successful strategic re-orientation. The order of priorities was, first, to depoliticise the army; second, to secure the military's loyalty to the new

74

government by civilianising the Ministries of Defence; and third, to end all ties with the former Warsaw Pact.

These efforts had varying degrees of success. The legislative powers of the new parliaments in creating the legal framework necessary to oversee the military, and even their influence on defence policy, have proved successful. In terms of their fiscal powers, however, the record so far is far less promising. The policy of civilianising the executive can be, and has been, criticised, above all because of the lack of civilian expertise in both military and public administration. Despite the failures, implementing these policies was enough to prove the governments' commitment to democratic control of the military independently of their other democratic policies. It is essential for the two policies of establishing democratic civilian control of the military and of Western integration to have the equal commitment of the political leadership under all circumstances, at all times. Subordinating one to the other will only create as many problems as it solves.

Domestic and international political developments in 1993–95, however, began to have a different impact on the relationship between these two policy goals. In 1993, Poland held its *Sejm* elections which resulted in victory for the former Communist Party, the Czech Republic and Slovakia became independent states, and Vladimir Meciar's leftist-nationalist HZDS came to power. In 1994, the general elections in Hungary returned the former Communist Party to government, and NATO's Partnership for Peace programme was launched, increasing the emphasis on civilian control of the military. In 1995, the presidential elections in Poland led to the ousting of the anti-communist Walesa by the former communist candidate. This significant shift to the left in the domestic political scene thus coincided with NATO's new approach to civilian control of the military, which it defined as one of the prime requirements for eastward enlargement.

Hungary is a 'model' example of the effect this shift had on civilian control of the military, which began to be seen as necessary for integration into Western security structures. The policy thus appears to have been introduced more as a concession than a political commitment. The electoral victory of the former Communist Party in 1994 meant the nomination of a retired colonel as Minister of Defence and a sweeping personnel change in the Ministry. In effect, it heralded the return or promotion to senior positions of many of the older generation of the military at the expense of an overwhelming number of civilian employees. Domestic and Western criticism of this change was great.

Under these pressures, the government gradually changed its policy: many of these older military personnel were retired into civilian-hood but remained in their Ministry of Defence positions, while others were forbidden from using their military rank or uniforms. Neither Hungary's former Communist Party nor that of Poland – elected in 1993 – had shown much commitment to democratic principles before 1989. On their return to power, they inherited the policy goals of Western integration and of civilian control over the military from the first post-Warsaw Pact governments. Ironically, their predecessors prior to 1989 had used control over the army as a means of consolidating their power for 40 years. There are many indications that civilian control has become a function of the policy of Western integration.

The increasing authoritarianism of Slovak Prime Minister Meciar subordinated the policy of civilian control to Western integration, as in Poland and Hungary. In Slovakia, this raises two fundamental issues. On the one hand, the voices supporting Slovak national independence had first surfaced within the Czechoslovak military. The difference in status between the Czech and Slovak professional corps, with Czech officers holding most of the senior positions, had caused conflict between the two ethnic groups. The military's campaign for an independent Slovak Army was soon accompanied by demands for independence from Slovak politicians to the extent that ethnic conflict among the ranks and in the entire country became a higher priority than the de-communisation of the army itself.[4] On the other hand, there has been no fundamental change in the Slovak political elite as in Poland or Hungary since the end of the Cold War.[5]

Besides subordinating civilian control to the policy of Western integration, the rise of the political left was, according to most opinion polls, supported by the military in Central Europe, and in some cases even contributed to the military's political assertiveness. Although the lack of civilian expertise in defence matters also contributed to the military's more active role in the policy process in Central Europe, the initial 'trespass' of the officer corps into policy has been attributed to the military.[6] The officer corps took advantage of weaknesses in the legislative framework and of conflicts among the civilian staff to secure their influence. In so doing, they subordinated the social imperative to their professional interest.[7] Political involvement of the military increased and civilian control diminished following the 1993 *Sejm* elections in Poland and the 1994 elections in Hungary. After Slovakia's independence, there was no official policy to involve civilians in defence matters, leaving the Ministry of Defence in the hands of the military.

The Implications of Limited Reforms

It is legitimate to ask how much it matters in the end whether the pledge behind establishing civilian control of the military is genuine or not, or whether these policies are pursued as a commitment or as a concession. There is a case to be made that as long as democratic civilian control of the military remains a requirement for cooperation with the West, it will continue to exercise positive pressure on Central and Eastern European governments.

There are two mid-term risks inherent in this thinking. First, if the policy approach towards civilian control of the military is that it will result in integration with the West, only those governments that deem their own chances of integration reasonable are likely to undertake serious reforms. Slovakia is a case in point. Its chances of being included in the 'first round' of NATO enlargement have been constantly decreasing.

Second, if establishing civilian control over the military is seen primarily as a peculiarity of Western interest, efforts are likely to concentrate on the 'visible' aspects of control, leaving the implementation untouched. This is the kind of Central and Eastern European government attitude that may have led many Western experts to conclude that the introduction of civilian control stagnates on the legal level, thus drawing attention to the superficial character of reforms.

These developments risk producing wide-ranging and self-perpetuating negative consequences. The actual policies implemented can easily remain minimalist and superficial. While civilian oversight can be only as deep and as wide as is necessary for successful Western integration, the political rhetoric of civilian control is not likely to diminish. If this remains unchallenged, the rift between policy goals and realities is bound to increase over time. It will entrench the conviction that rather than profound reforms, what really matters is good rhetoric. In addition, actually 'implementing' the principle of civilian control may remain in the hands of the military. There are already signs that the lack of consensus between civilians and military in Central Europe is becoming an everyday reality. This is likely to strengthen further the positions and attitudes of the older generation of officers. Throughout Central Europe, this older generation accepted the need for political commitment for 40 years as a way of protecting their interests, and subordinating civilian control to the policy of Western integration may re-invigorate the informal ties between the political and the military spheres. The military has gained, or managed to retain, opportunities to exert passive resistance and engage in behind-the-scenes political manoeuvres, leading to the stalling of reform efforts deemed contrary to military interests.

Another potential risk is the re-intrusion of the political sphere into the military one. Protecting the political structure from military intervention is just one of the goals of civilian control of the military. Its counterpart, protecting the military from being used by partisan politics, has not been fully accomplished and haunts civil–military relations in Central Europe. Following the shift in the role of this relationship, the risk of those in power influencing the military for partisan politics has grown considerably. Legal reforms could only influence the formal ties between the military and the former communist parties in Central Europe after 1989–90. The military, on the level of pronouncements, accepted the principle of civilian dominance in all countries. Yet informal ties survived the reforms and restrictions, and in many cases re-surfaced after the former communist parties were re-elected in Central Europe. Voting patterns reveal the persistence of old political ties and sympathies among the older generation.

The combination of these factors points to the conclusion that the older generation of the professional officer corps in Central Europe never really withdrew from politics. Their passive resistance to the new reforms has been seen in many Central European countries, together with concealed obstructionism and, on some occasions, even open siding with one or another political actor. The heritage of behind-the-scenes political involvement is deeply ingrained, and is still alive and well among the older generation of Central Europe's officer corps. After 1989–90, a rift appeared between the older and younger military officers, as the younger ones began to support increasing military professionalisation and civilian control. But as long as the older generation retain their positions, the younger generation cannot support the reforms.

A more latent risk, implied by the shift in the role of civil–military relations in Central Europe, is that most military restructuring can be carried out more efficiently based on the informal ties between the military and the old-new political leadership. In addition, several aspects of reform can be presented as increasing civilian control of the military, but the line between civilian control and partisan political influence over the army can all too easily become elastic.

Promoting democratic civil–military relations is becoming more of a tactic than a genuine strategy of reform in Central Europe, and there is a continuing discrepancy between the structures and reality of civilian oversight. The Soviet military heritage is deeply rooted in Central Europe's officer corps. The Communist Party's long influence over the military cannot be simply eliminated through legal measures, by abolishing certain institutions and establishing new ones. Democracy itself is a process, and profound changes take time to take root. The more optimistic analysts of civil–military relations in Central Europe tend to de-emphasise, however, that implementing these reforms requires just as much political commitment as did setting up the legal framework in the first place.

If it is true that armed forces reflect the values of the society in which they function and are shaped by those values far more than by external threats to society (especially when there is no such imminent threat), then loss of sincerity in the democratisation process is bound to produce mid-term risks. Many subtle but nevertheless tangible signs point to the gradual subordination of one policy goal to the other, as analysed in this paper. The process of establishing civilian control has been further aggravated by a chronic lack of civilian expertise in defence matters and of independent strategic communities in the region. These factors pose a challenge to Western interests in re-thinking policies aimed at promoting transparency and civilianisation of defence decision-making in Central Europe.

Subordinating the policy of civilian control over the military to that of Western integration directly affects Western democracies. In the first period of reforms, when the two goals were of equal importance, Western assistance in promoting civil–military relations was primarily technical and tactical. As a result of domestic political shifts in Central Europe, Western support for establishing democratic civilian control of the military is becoming of strategic importance if real and sustained democratic and civilian control of the armed forces is to be established there. The serious reform efforts of the first generation of the political elite in Central Europe succeeded in placing these countries in the vanguard of political reforms. As the reforms of civil–military relations have been stalled and/or subsequently 'forfeited' to other political considerations, a new wave of Western support focusing on training civilians is urgently required for genuine civilianisation and democratisation of Central European defence policy.

NOTES

Introduction

[1] See Thomas S. Szayna and F. Stephen Larrabee, *East European Military Reform After the Cold War: Implications for the US* (Santa Monica, CA: RAND, 1995), p. 26.

[2] For two excellent studies, see Jeffrey Simon, *NATO Enlargement and Central Europe: A Study in Civil–Military Relations* (Washington DC: National Defense University Press, 1996), and Rudolf Joo, *The Democratic Control of Armed Forces*, Chaillot Paper 23 (Paris: Western European Union Institute for Security Studies, 1996).

Chapter I

[1] Louis Smith, *American Democracy and Military Power* (New York: Arno Press, 1979).

[2] For a comparison with the former Soviet Union, see Robert Barylski, *Perestroika and Civil–Military Relations in the Soviet Union and in the People's Republic of China*, Forum International 14 (Munich: Sozialwissenschaftliches Institut der Bundeswehr (SOWI), 1992).

[3] On the various types of military involvement in politics, see Constantine P. Danopoulos (ed.), *Military Disengagement from Politics* (London and New York: Routledge, 1988). Western Europe's experience of the military in politics and the factors necessary for successful military coups in a democracy are also of interest. For example, the French Army supported General de Gaulle's rise to power and then came close to toppling his government in the 1950s, while in Greece, the Army seized power in 1967 and held on to it until as late as 1974.

[4] See Ivan Volgyes, *The Political Reliability of the Warsaw Pact Armies: The Southern Tier*, Duke Press Policy Studies (Durham, NC: Duke University Press, 1982), p. 6.

[5] For an insightful conceptualisation of communist-type civil–military relations, see Dale R. Herspring and Ivan Volgyes (eds), *Civil–Military Relations in Communist Systems* (Boulder, CO: Westview, 1978).

[6] See more in Roman Kolkowicz, *The Soviet Military and the Communist Party* (Princeton, NJ: Princeton University Press, 1967), and William E. Odom, *Commissars, Commanders and Civilian Authority: The Structure of Soviet Military Politics* (Cambridge, MA: Harvard University Press, 1979).

[7] Zoltan Barany, 'East European Armed Forces in Transition and Beyond', *East European Quarterly* vol. 26, no. 1, Spring 1992, pp. 1–30.

[8] For more on the tensions between the civilian Ministers of Defence and the officer corps, see Szayna and Larrabee, *East European*

Military Reform After the Cold War, pp. 23–26.

[9] Ferenc Gazdag, 'Difficult Inheritance: The Relationship Between the Armed Forces and Civilian Organisations in Central and Eastern Europe – A Hungarian Perspective', paper presented to the seminar 'Military Assistance to Civilian Authorities in Democracies', NATO Defence College, Rome, 7–9 December 1995, p. 6; Bartosz Weglarczyk, 'The Military and the Media: The Polish Case', paper presented to the IISS workshop, 'Civil–Military Relations in Central Europe', Budapest, 23–24 March 1996; and Stefan Sarvas, *The Professional Corps in Central and Eastern European Politics* (Groningen: Centre for European Security Studies, 1995).

[10] Tamas Fellegi, 'Regime Transformation and Mid-level Bureaucratic Forces in Hungary', in Peter Volten (ed.), *Bound to Change: Consolidating Democracy in East Central Europe* (New York: Institute of East–West Studies, 1992).

[11] Marie Vlahova and Stefan Sarvas, 'From the Totalitarian to the Post-Totalitarian Military', in Anton A. Bebler (ed.), *Civil–Military Relations in Post-Communist States* (Westport, CT: Greenwood, 1995), p. 8.

[12] For example, General Pezl was appointed Chief of the General Staff and General Greiner was appointed Head of Personnel, whereas Antonin Rasek, a civilian, was appointed First Deputy Minister of Defence and Head of the Department of Education and Culture.

[13] Directorate of Management and Consultancy Services, UK Ministry of Defence, *Review of Parliamentary Oversight of the Hungarian Ministry of Defence and Democratic Control of the Hungarian Armed Forces*, D/MAN S (ORG)/60/Study 810 (London: Ministry of Defence, 1996). (Emphasis added.)

[14] Jeffrey Simon, 'Forging a Civilian Chain of Command for Poland's Military', *Transition*, 15 December 1995, p. 40.

[15] See more in Smith, *American Democracy and Military Power*, and Charles Rose, 'Democratic Control of the Armed Forces: A Parliamentary Role in Partnership for Peace', *NATO Review*, vol.??, no. 5, October 1994, pp. 13–17.

[16] See Smith, *American Democracy and Military Power*.

[17] Joo, *The Democratic Control of Armed Forces*, p. 26.

[18] This seems of most concern to Czech and Hungarian members of parliament.

Chapter II

[1] These views were expressed most explicitly by Czech policy-makers.

[2] This was highlighted in 1995 by Andrew Cottey, *East-Central Europe after the Cold War: Poland, the Czech Republic, Slovakia and Hungary in Search of Security*

(New York: St Martin's Press, 1995), p. 124.

[3] In 1993 in Hungary, for instance, according to a member of parliament, the only weapons purchased were a few thousand hand grenades.

[4] Janos Szabo, *Ismeretlen es Ismert Elemek a NATO-Csatlakozas Egyenlet-Rendszereben* (Budapest: Zrinyi Miklos Military Academy (ZMKA), 1996). A recent sociological study argues that 36% of the population supports 'a significant pay-rise' for the officer corps, and concludes that there is little evidence that the public wishes to decrease the GNP percentage of the defence budget.

[5] Open Media Research Institute, Radio Free Europe/Radio Liberty, *Daily Report*, 16 July 1996.

[6] UK Ministry of Defence, *Review of Parliamentary Oversight of the Hungarian Ministry of Defence and Democratic Control of the Hungarian Armed Forces*, p. 5.

[7] Janusz Onyszkiewicz, *Civil–Military Relations in Poland* (Washington DC: International Forum for Democratic Studies, 1996).

[8] An example of the imbalance of power in favour of the executive is the modernisation of MiG-21s in the Czech Republic. The Parliamentary Security Committee was still discussing the project when the Ministry of Defence began to implement it.

[9] A detailed description of PPBS can be found in Frantisek Ochrana,

'The Ministry of Defence Planning, Programming and Budgeting System of the Czech Republic', paper presented to the IISS workshop, 'Civil–Military Relations in Central Europe', Budapest, 23–24 March 1996.

[10] Interview, January 1996.

[11] Jiry Kuchyna: 'The Making of the Defence Budget – The Czech Experience', paper presented to the IISS workshop, 'Civil–Military Relations in Central Europe', Budapest, 23–24 March 1996.

[12] *Ibid.*

[13] Interview with Vladimir Suman, Chairman of the Defence and Security Committee, Prague, January 1996.

[14] Interview with Peter Vetrecili, Economic Department, Slovak Ministry of Defence, February 1996.

[15] Interview with Stefan Baxa, Defence and Security Committee, Slovak Parliament, February 1996.

[16] Roman Zatko, 'Civil–Military Relations Within the Framework of Western Integration', paper presented to the IISS workshop, 'Civil–Military Relations in Central Europe', Budapest, 23–24 March 1996.

[17] Sandor Turjan, 'Planning Defence Expenditure', paper presented to the IISS workshop, 'Civil–Military Relations in Central Europe', Budapest, 23–24 March 1996.

[18] Interview with Sandor Turjan, Budapest, March 1996.

[19] UK Ministry of Defence, *Review of Parliamentary Oversight of the*

Hungarian Ministry of Defence and Democratic Control of the Hungarian Defence Forces, p. 22.

Chapter III

[1] In Simon, *NATO Enlargement and Central Europe*, and Simon, 'Forging a Chain of Civilian Command for Poland's Military', pp. 37–40.

[2] See David R. Segal, 'Civil–Military Relations in Democratic Societies', in James A. Kuhlman and Segal (eds), *Armed Forces at the Dawn of the Third Millenium*, Forum International 16 (Munich: SOWI, 1992).

[3] For Hungary, see Janos Szabo, 'Facts and Problems of the Civilian Control of Armed Forces in Hungary', paper presented to the IISS workshop, 'Civil–Military Relations in Central Europe', Budapest, 23–24 March 1996, p. 5. For Slovakia, see Eduard Mracka, 'View of the Role of The Military Leadership', paper presented to the IISS workshop, 'Civil–Military Relations in Central Europe', Budapest, 23–24 March 1996, p. 1.

[4] On the importance of this principle in Central Europe, see Szayna and Larrabee, *East European Military Reform After the Cold War*.

[5] See more in Michael Sadykiewicz and Louisa Vinton, 'Politicization and the Polish Military', *Report on Eastern Europe*, 30 March 1990.

[6] Zoltan D. Barany, *Soldiers and Politics in Eastern Europe: 1945–1990: The Case of Hungary* (New York: St Martin's Press, 1993), p. 119.

[7] *Magyar Közlöny*, no. 59, Budapest, 25 June 1990, pp. 1,269–79.

[8] The verb 'to lustrate' comes from the Latin *lustrum*, an act of purification by sacrifice.

[9] Vlahova and Sarvas, 'From the Totalitarian to the Post-Totalitarian Military', p. 11.

[10] F. Harris, 'Thousands of Czech Officers Leave Forces in "Loyalty" Protest', *Report on Eastern Europe*, 6 April 1990, p. 12, quoted in Cottey, *East-Central Europe after the Cold War*, p. 74.

[11] *Democratic Control Over Security Policy and Armed Forces* (Prague: Institute of International Relations, 1995), p. 44.

[12] Cottey, *East-Central Europe after the Cold War*, p. 120.

[13] On the theory of 'loose coupling' in the Soviet era, see Brian A. Davenport, 'Civil–Military Relations in the Post-Soviet State: "Loose Coupling" Uncoupled?', *Armed Forces and Society*, vol. 21, no. 2, Winter 1995, pp. 175–94.

[14] Samuel Huntington, *The Soldier and the State* (Cambridge, MA: Harvard University Press, 1957).

[15] Samuel Sarkesian argues that the discrepancy between theory (that armed forces are apolitical) and reality (that they are not) shows ignorance of both history and reality. See Sarkesian, 'Military Professionalism and Civil–Military Relations in the West', *International Science Review*, vol.

2, no. 3, 1981. Samuel Finer argues in *The Man on Horseback: The Role of the Military in Politics* (Boulder, CO: Westview, 1988) that lobbying, as the articulation of professional interest, is almost part of professional duty. Martin Edmonds points out in *Armed Services and Society* (Boulder, CO: Westview, 1990) that the fact that armed forces are involved in politics is not a value judgement but a factual statement.

[16] Morris Janowitz, *The Professional Soldier: A Social and Political Portrait* (New York: Free Press, 1971).

[17] In the Czech Republic, the first official document setting out the future development of the Czech military is the *Military Strategy Plan to 2005* (Prague: Ministry of Defence, 1994).

[18] *Democratic Control Over Security Policy and Armed Forces*, p. 30.

[19] Szabo, 'Facts and Problems of the Civilian Control of Armed Forces in Hungary', pp. 7–8.

[20] One of the most interesting examples occurred during the American Civil War, expressed by Emory Upton. See Eliot A. Cohen, *Making Do With Less, Or Coping With Upton's Ghost* (Carlisle, PA: US Army War College, Strategic Studies Institute, May 1995).

[21] See more on the Hungarian military's case in Alfred A. Reisch, *The Hungarian Army in Transition*, Radio Free Europe/Radio Liberty, *Research Report*, 5 March 1993.

[22] On the Czech Army's present and future, see the *White Paper on Defence of the Czech Republic, 1995* (Prague: Ministry of Defence, 1995).

[23] For Hungary, see Pal Dunay, *After the System Change: Hungary in the New European Security System* (Budapest: Department of International Law, Eotvos University, 1992). For the considerations and concerns surrounding the Soviet military's withdrawal, see Henry Plater-Zyberk, *The Soviet Military Withdrawal From Central Europe* (London: Brassey's for the Centre for Defence Studies, 1991).

[24] The then Czechoslovak Army's contribution to the Gulf War was a chemical platoon; the Hungarian Army's was a medical unit.

[25] *Democratic Control Over Security Policy and Armed Forces*, p. 49.

[26] This was one of the conclusions of the UK Ministry of Defence's *Review of Parliamentary Oversight of the Hungarian Ministry of Defence and Democratic Control of the Hungarian Defence Forces.*

[27] Szabo, 'Facts and Problems of the Civilian Control of Armed Forces in Hungary', p. 10.

[28] Stefan Sarvas, 'The Changed Role of the Military in Society', paper presented to the IISS workshop, 'Civil–Military Relations in Central Europe', Budapest, 23–24 March 1996, p. 6.

[29] For the Czechoslovak data, see *Democratic Control Over Security*

Policy and Armed Forces, p. 57. For the Hungarian data, see Gazdag, 'Difficult Inheritance'.

[30] Laszlo Szabo, 'Fostering Civil–Military Relations: The Case of Hungary', paper delivered at a Joint SOWI–Inter-University Seminar (IUS) Conference, 'Fostering Democratic Civil–Military Relations', Strausberg, Germany, 8–12 June 1996.

[31] This has caused a lot of problems, especially in the Czech Republic.

[32] Ferenc Molnár, *A Magyar Honvédség Civil Kontrolljának Helyzete és Lehetõségei* (Budapest: ZMKA, February 1996).

[33] Marie Vlahova and Stefan Sarvas, 'Fostering Civil–Military Relations: The Case of the Czech Republic', paper presented at a joint SOWI-IUS Conference, 'Fostering Democratic Civil–Military Relations', Strausberg, Germany, 8–12 June 1996.

[34] Vlahova and Sarvas, 'From the Totalitarian to the Post-Totalitarian Military', p. 11. Similar polls have been conducted in Slovakia, but are not publicly available.

[35] Vlahova and Sarvas, 'Fostering Civil–Military Relations: The Case of the Czech Republic'.

[36] Interview in the Personnel Department of the Czech Ministry of Defence, January 1996.

[37] Szabó, 'Fostering Civil–Military Relations: The Case of Hungary'.

[38] Vlahova and Sarvas, 'From the Totalitarian to the Post-Totalitarian Military', p. 12.

[39] For instance, it was 57% in 1996.

See Molnar, *A Magyar Honvédség Civil Kontrolljának Helyzete és Lehetõségei*, p. 15.

[40] Vlahova and Sarvas, 'Fostering Civil–Military Relations: The Case of the Czech Republic', pp. 13–15.

[41] Janos Szabo, *A Hivatásos Tisztek és Tiszthelyettesek NATO-Csatlakozással Kapcsolatos Beállitódásai* (Budapest: ZMKA, 1996), pp. 10, 16, 24.

[42] Act 361/1992 regulates this.

[43] Interview with former Defence Minister Onyszkiewicz of Poland.

[44] Thirteen for the Non-Party Bloc Supporting Reforms, two for the Coalition for the Republic, two for the Democratic Left Alliance and six for the Polish Peasant Party.

[45] See Sir Michael Howard, 'Military Education: The Tasks Ahead', in Ernest Gilman and Detlef Herold (eds), *The Role of Military Education in the Armed Forces* (Rome: NATO Defence College, 1993), pp. 137–46.

Chapter IV

[1] Because of the difficulty of finding comparable statistics, polls taken in the four countries provide the basis for comparison here.

[2] See Andrzej Korbonski and Sarah M. Terry, 'The Military as Political Actor in Poland', in Roman Kolkowicz and Andrzej Korbonski (eds), *Soldiers, Peasants, and Bureaucrats – Civil–Military Relations in Communist and Modernising Societies* (London and Boston, MA: G. Allen and Unwin, 1982).

[3] Stefan Sarvas, *Civil–Military Relations in the Czech Republic*, (Prague: Institute of International Relations, October 1995).

[4] See more on Slovak history in Stanislav J. Kirschbaum, *A History of Slovakia: The Struggle for Survival* (New York: St Martin's Press, 1995), and Judy Batt, *Czechoslovakia in Transition: From Federation to Separation* (London: Royal Institute of International Affairs, 1993).

[5] Interview with Col. Vladimir Kmec, Ministry of Defence, Bratislava, May 1996.

[6] Eduard Mracka, 'The Role of The Military Leadership', paper presented to the IISS workshop, 'Civil–Military Relations in Central Europe', Budapest, 23–24 March 1996, p. 6.

[7] Daniela Geisbacherova, 'Civil–Military Relations and the Process of Democratization in the Slovak Republic', talk given at the George C. Marshall Centre, Garmisch-Partenkirchen, Germany, pp. 4–5.

[8] Vlahova and Sarvas, 'From the Totalitarian to the Post-Totalitarian Military'.

[9] Interview with Major Balaban, Ministry of Defence, Prague, January 1996.

[10] Geisbacherova, 'Civil–Military Relations and the Process of Democratization in the Slovak Republic', pp. 4–5.

[11] Molnar, *A Magyar Honvédség Civil Kontrolljának Helyzete és Lehetōségei*, p. 15, and Hungarian Ministry of Defence, *A Honvédelem*

Négy Éve 1990–1994 (Budapest: Zrinyi Kiado, 1994), p. 129.

[12] Molnar, *A Magyar Honvédség Civil Kontrolljának Helyzete és Lehetōségei*, p. 15.

[13] Adam Kolodziejczyk, 'The Importance of Conscription versus Voluntary Service in Poland', paper delivered at a Joint SOWI–IUS Conference, 'Fostering Democratic Civil–Military Relations', Strausberg, Germany, 8–12 June 1996.

[14] See more in Bartosz Weglarcyk, 'The Military and the Media: The Polish Case'.

[15] *Právo*, for instance, favoured by left-wingers, usually has a more critical tone than *Denní Telegraf*, the paper favoured by the Civic Democratic Party.

[16] General Wileczki, a Walesa appointee.

[17] Polish Ministry of Defence, Warsaw, 1996.

[18] The right to information in the Czech Republic is guaranteed in the Charter of Essential Rights and Liberties, and is fine-tuned in the Press Act.

[19] See UK Ministry of Defence, *Review of Parliamentary Oversight of the Hungarian Ministry of Defence and Democratic Control of the Hungarian Defence Forces*, p. 57.

[20] Vlahova and Sarvas, 'Fostering Civil–Military Relations: The Czech Case'.

[21] Henryk Dziewluski, 'Selected Issues of Civil–Military Relations in Poland', paper delivered at a

Joint SOWI–IUS Conference, 'Fostering Democratic Civil–Military Relations', Strausberg, Germany, 8–12 June 1996.

Chapter V
[1] For an excellent analysis of the various institutions in Western models of civilian control, see Joo, *The Democratic Control of Armed Forces*, pp. 8–11.
[2] See more in F. Stephen Larrabee, *East European Security After the Cold War* (Santa Monica, CA: RAND, 1993).
[3] See Simon, 'Forging a Chain of Civilian Command for Poland's Military', pp. 37–40.
[4] *A National Security Strategy of Engagement and Enlargement* (Washington DC: The White House, 1994).
[5] Marian Kowalewski, personal communication, and remarks by Ferenc Gazdag, Budapest, spring 1996.
[6] On the military focus of PFP, see James C. Oliphant, 'Partnership for Peace – A Progress Report', Conflict Studies Research Centre, Royal Military Academy, Sandhurst, Camberley, Surrey, March 1996.
[7] For example, the US International Military Education and Training (IMET) courses. See John A. Cope, *International Military Education and Training: An Assessment,* McNair Paper 44 (Washington DC: Institute for National Strategic Studies, National Defense University, October 1995). See also Rose, 'Democratic Control of the Armed Forces', pp. 13–17.
[8] Cohen, *Making Do With Less, Or Coping With Upton's Ghost.*
[9] See Christopher Donnelly, 'Developing a National Strategy for the Transformation of the Defence Establishment in Post-Communist Societies', *European Security*, vol. 5, no. 1, Spring 1996, pp. 1–15.
[10] See more in Donald Abenheim, *Reforging the Iron Cross: The Search for Tradition in the West German Armed Forces* (Princeton, NJ: Princeton University Press, 1988).

Conclusion
[1] For more on the Central European security concerns, 1990–92, see Jan Zielonka, *Security in Central Europe,* Adelphi Paper 272 (London: Brassey's for the IISS, 1992).
[2] Cottey, *East-Central Europe after the Cold War*, pp. 73–75.
[3] Barany, 'East European Armed Forces in Tranisiotn and Beyond', pp. 1–30, argues rightly that there was no military threat from the military in either Poland or Hungary. For Poland, see Louisa Vinton, 'Domestic Politics and Foreign Policy, 1989–1993', in Ilya Prizel and Andrew A. Michta (eds), *Polish Foreign Policy Reconsidered: Challenges of Independence* (London: Macmillan, 1995), pp. 23–72. On the role of the military see D. M. Perry, *A New Military Lobby,* Radio Free Europe/Radio Liberty, *Research Report*, 5

October 1990, p. 3.

[4] Thomas S. Szayna: *The Military in Post-Communist Czechoslovakia* (Santa Monica, CA: RAND,1992), and Szayna and James B. Steinberg, *Civil–Military Relations and National Security Thinking in Czechoslovakia: A Conference Report* (Santa Monica, CA: RAND, 1992), already warned that ethnic conflict in the Czechoslovak Army could ultimately lead to the break-up of the state.

[5] Sona Szomolanyi, 'Old Elites in the New Slovak State and Their Current Transformations', in Szomolanyi and G. Meseznikov (eds), *The Slovak Path of Transition – To Democracy?* (Bratislava: Slovak Political Science Association and Interlingua, 1994), pp. 67–86.

[6] Sarvas, 'The Changed Role of the Military in Society'.

[7] Huntington, *The Soldier and The State*.

APPENDIX

Major political events in Czechoslovakia, the Czech Republic, Hungary, Poland and Slovakia from 1989 to mid-1996.

CZECHOSLOVAKIA

November 1989 Street demonstrations bring down communist government.
Country renamed Czechoslovak Federal Republic.

December 1989 Marian Calfa appointed Prime Minister by Communist Party.
Vaclav Havel elected President by Federal Assembly.
Association of Military Renewal (SVO) established by former military officers dismissed after 1968.
Obroda (Renewal) military union formed.
Gen. Miroslav Vacek becomes new Minister of Defence; abolishes Communist Party organisations within the military; Antonin Rasek becomes first civilian Deputy Minister of Defence; Karel Pezl appointed new Chief of General Staff.

January 1990 Calfa becomes first post-communist Prime Minister.
Union of Professional Soldiers established.

April 1990 Country renamed Czech and Slovak Federal Republic.

June 1990 First free elections held.

September 1990 Minister of Defence Vacek dismissed for involvement in Operation Wave against anti-communist demonstrators.

October 1990 Lubos Dobrovsky becomes first civilian Minister of Defence.

December 1990 Act dividing functions between Prague and Bratislava passed.

January 1991 Charter of Fundamental Rights and Freedoms.
Association of Slovak Soldiers established.

May 1992 Vladimir Meciar, head of Slovakia's Movement for a Democratic Slovakia (HZDS), tells Havel that Slovakia will declare sovereignty, adopt a new Constitution and hold a referendum on remaining in the Federation.

| June 1992 | Calfa's government resigns; Jan Strasky (Civic Democratic Party, ODS) forms new government; Lt-Gen. Imrich Andrejcak appointed Minister of Defence at Meciar's insistence. Ensuing unresolvable tensions bring the Czech and Slovak Federal Republic to its end. |

THE CZECH REPUBLIC

June 1992	Coalition government formed by ODS, Christian Democratic Union– Czechoslovak People's Party (KDU–CSL) and Civic Democratic Alliance (ODA), with 76, 15 and 14 seats respectively.
December 1992	Independent Czech Constitution adopted.
January 1993	Declaration of independence of the Czech Republic. Vaclav Havel elected President. Antonin Baudys (KDU) appointed first Minister of Defence.
May 1993	Political screening of 28,000 members of the professional military starts.
July 1993	Jiri Nekvasil named new Chief of the General Staff.
March 1994	Partnership for Peace (PFP) General Agreement signed.
May 1994	Country becomes Associate Member of Western European Union (WEU).
September 1994	Vilem Holan (KDU–CSL) becomes second Minister of Defence.
January 1995	Army adopts Planning, Programming and Budgetary System (PPBS).
November 1995	Country becomes full members of Organisation for Economic Cooperation and Development (OECD).
January 1996	Country submits official application for membership of European Union.
March 1996	Inter-agency NATO Integration Committee established.
May/June 1996	Prime Minister Vaclav Klaus forms minority government (99 out of 200 seats) with ODS, KDU–CSL and ODA; opposition Social Democrat Milos Zeman (CSSD) becomes parliamentary speaker; Miloslav Vyborny (KDU–CSL) appointed third Minister of Defence.

July 1989	Communist Party (MSZMP) Committee on the People's Army dissolves itself; Party cells within the Army are dissolved.
Summer 1989	Prime Minister Miklos Nemeth forms caretaker government.
September 1989	'Iron curtain' raised in Hungary for East German refugees.
October 1989	Republic of Hungary proclaimed.
December 1989	Separation of General Staff from Ministry of Defence to retain MSZMP control over the military.
March 1990	Parliament modifies Constitution and National Defence Act; designates President as Commander-in-Chief; People's Army renamed Home Defence Forces (HDF); General Staff (responsible to President) legally separated from the Ministry of Defence (responsible to government). Jozsef Antall forms centre-right coalition government of Hungarian Democratic Forum (MDF), Christian Democratic People's Party (KDNP) and Independent Smallholders (FKGP).
May 1990	Lajos Fur becomes first civilian Minister of Defence in Central and Eastern Europe.
1990–91	Serious tension develops between coalition government and opposition.
August 1990	Opposition member Arpad Goncz elected President.
March 1993	New civilian Administrative State Secretary appointed in Ministry of Defence.
April 1993	Resolution 27 passed on Basic National Defence Principles.
November 1993	Parliament approves new Defence Law to merge Ministry of Defence and General Staff; Chief of General Staff becomes directly subordinated to Minister of Defence.
December 1993	Prime Minister Antall dies; caretaker government remains in power under Prime Minister Boross.
February 1994	PFP General Agreement signed.
May 1994	Prime Minister Gyula Horn elected from Hungarian Socialist Party (successor to the MSZMP) with 54% of seats; forms coalition government with left-liberal

Alliance of Free Democrats (18% of seats). Retired Col. Gyorgy Keleti becomes Minister of Defence.

Coalition Chairman of Parliamentary Defence Committee Mecs warns of the 'militarisation' of the Ministry of Defence.

mid-1994   Serious financial problems result from decline in the defence budget.

November 1994 Top two military positions (Chief of General Staff and Commander of the HDF) separated again.

January 1995 Armaments Reform Concept presented to parliament to reflect goal of NATO integration, but determined by extremely tight defence budget.

May 1996   Posts of Chief of General Staff and Commander of the HDF combined again with appointment of Lt.-Gen. Ferenc Vegh (trained in US Army War College).

June 1996   NATO Integration Department established in Ministry of Defence.

July 1996   Maj.-Gen Lajos Fodor appointed new First Deputy Chief of Staff (trained in US National War College)

POLAND

Spring 1989   Round-table talks between government (PUWR) and opposition.

June 1989   General elections for only 35% of *Sejm* seats, but all of Senate seats; PUWP defeated in Senate and loses majority in *Sejm*; sweeping victory for *Solidarnosc.*

August 1989   Tadeusz Mazowiecki elected first non-communist Prime Minister.

Active Gen. Florian Siwicki appointed Minister of Defence.

Wojciech Jaruzelski elected President by small parliamentary majority.

September 1989 Senate re-established.

April 1990   Civilians Bronislaw Komorowski and Janusz Onyszkiewicz appointed Deputy Ministers of Defence.

July 1990   Adm. Piotr Kolodziejczyk becomes new Minister of Defence; voices increasingly anti-Soviet views.

October 1990	Gen. Z. Stelmaszuk appointed Chief of General Staff.
December 1990	Lech Walesa wins presidential election.
January 1991	Jan Bielecki appointed second non-communist Prime Minister.
	Adm. Kolodziejczyk becomes Minister of Defence (for second time)
Spring 1991	Deputy Minister of Defence Onyszkiewicz outlines defence reform concept for Ministry of Defence and General Staff.
	President Walesa announces will appoint civilian Minister of Defence.
	Inter-ministerial reform commission set up to civilianise Ministry of Defence, restructure armed forces, rationalise defence industry and establish military oversight.
	Tensions appear between communist majority *Sejm* and *Solidarnosc*-held Senate, and between parliament and President Walesa.
October 1991	First full, democratic *Sejm* and Senate elections result in very fragmented parliament (29 parties in *Sejm*).
	Jan Olszewski becomes third Prime Minister; tensions between him and Walesa heighten.
January 1992	Jan Parys becomes first civilian Minister of Defence; dismisses Deputy Minister Komorowski; Deputy Minister Onyszkiewicz resigns.
April 1992	Minister Parys accuses President of planning to introduce Martial Law; accusation rebuffed, Parys resigns; Olszewski government falls.
June 1992	Waldemar Pawlak becomes fourth Prime Minister.
	Onyszkiewicz appointed Minister of Defence, begins to reform Ministry; wishes to restore good relations with President.
July 1992	Hanna Suchocka becomes fifth Prime Minister.
August 1992	Gen. Tadeusz Wileczki, chosen by Walesa, becomes new Chief of General Staff reflecting improved relations between government and President.
March 1993	Restructuring of Ministry of Defence completed; next task to civilianise Ministry and redeploy personnel.

May 1993	Suchocka government falls by a small margin after vote of no-confidence.
September 1993	Minister of Defence Onyszkiewicz becomes subject of orchestrated criticism by highest-ranking military. Victory for Democratic Left Alliance (SLD, successor to PUWR) in *Sejm* and Senate elections with 208 seats out of 560; forms two-party coalition with Polish Peasant Party (PSL). Waldemar Pawlak (PSL) becomes 6th Prime Minister. President Walesa gains right to nominate Ministers of Defence, Foreign Affairs and Interior.
October 1993	Adm. Kolodziejczyk appointed Minister of Defence (for third time).
February 1994	Poland signs the PFP General Agreement and joins the programme. New Constitutional Committee chaired by Aleksander Kwasniewski set up to draft Constitution. Government promises to increase military budget, but parliament ends up decreasing it. Serious tensions between President and Minister of Defence Kolodziejczyk.
September 1994	So-called 'Drawsko Affair': President Walesa incites highest-ranking generals to criticise Minister Kolodziejczyk.
November 1994	Minister Kolodziejczyk dismissed; Jerzy Milewski becomes acting Minister of Defence. Defence budget for 1995 is 1.7% higher than for 1994 (for the first time since 1986).
January 1995	In his war against the SLD government, Walesa argues that the 'military should run the military'
February 1995	Civilian Z. Okonski becomes new Minister of Defence.
November 1995	Walesa defeated by SLD leader Aleksander Kwasniewski in presidential elections.
December 1995	Andrzej Karkoszka appointed acting Minister of Defence. Allegations made that SLD Prime Minister Jozef Oleksy collaborated with the KGB.
January 1996	Stanislaw Dobrzanski (PSL) becomes Minister of Defence.

February 1996	New Act on the Post of Minister of National Defence increases power of government by placing Chief of Staff, military prosecutors, courts and secret services under Minister of Defence's direct control.
	Prime Minister Oleksy resigns over spying scandal; replaced by Wlodzimierz Cimoszewicz (SLD).
April 1996	Military Prosecutor drops case against Oleksy for lack of evidence.
June 1996	Law on State Civil Service passed in attempt to create neutral professional civil service.
July 1996	Council of Minister approves decree on restructuring the Ministry of Defence to increase its responsibility, reduce its personnel and administrative structure and reduce number of generals to 120.

SLOVAKIA

July 1992	Slovak Parliament declares sovereignty.
September 1992	Slovak Constitution approved.
January 1993	Slovak Republic formed.
February 1993	Michal Kovac elected President; disputes within governing HZDS increase.
March 1993	Gen. Imrich Andrejcak appointed first Minister of Defence.
May 1993	National Security Council replaces State Defence Council.
October 1993	HZDS–Slovak National Party (SNS) coalition government formed.
February 1994	PFP General Agreement signed.
March 1994	Prime Minister Meciar's government ousted in a vote of no-confidence.
	Jozef Moravcik forms new government; Pavol Kanis appointed first civilian Minister of Defence.
August 1994	General Staff subordinated to Ministry of Defence in an effort to increase their cooperation.
	Government priority to solve increasing tensions between Ministry and Army Commander Gen. Julius Humaj.
September 1994	Minister of Defence plans to reduce size and restructure Ministry, as well as to move Army High

Command to General Staff.
Col.-Gen. Jozef Tuchyna becomes new Chief of
General Staff; Gen. Humaj becomes Deputy Chief
of General Staff.
Military reform introduced to transform regiment
structure into brigades in 1995.

October 1994   Moravcik defeated by Meciar in election.

December 1994 Meciar's HZDS forms coalition government with its
satellite Slovak Farmer's Party (RSS), Association
of Slovak Workers (ZRS) and extreme right SNS
(61, 13 and 9 seats respectively; total of 83 out of
150 seats).
Jan Sitek (SNS) becomes third Minister of Defence.

March 1995   Slovak–Hungarian Treaty on Good Neighbourly
Relations and Cooperation signed.

June 1995   Law on Military Service and Law on the Army of
the Slovak Republic amended; opposition protests
that these laws violate paras 102 and 119 of
Constitution.
Country submits official application to join EU.

August 1995   Michal Kovac Jr kidnapped; Slovak Information
Service (SIS) and Prime Minister Meciar himself
accused of involvement in abduction.

October 1995   EU and US express concern over political
developments in Slovakia and the kidnapping.

November 1995 Law on State Language is passed.

January 1996   Law on State Language strongly criticised by
Organisation for Security and Cooperation in
Europe (OSCE) Commissioner for National
Minorities Max van der Stoel.

March 1996   The first higher academic course begins at the
Slovak Military Academy.

May 1996   Defence Law amended to allow Slovak military
personnel to participate in international
peacekeeping operations.
Training of reservists resumes after five years.